AUGUSTINE: THE CONFESSIONS

Also available or forthcoming in this series:

AUGUSTINE: THE CONFESSIONS

Gillian Clark

BRISTOL
PHOENIX
PRESS

Cover illustration: based on *St Augustine*, by Sandro Botticelli,
Ognissanti, Florence

First published in 2005 by
Bristol Phoenix Press
Reed Hall, Streatham Drive
Exeter, Devon EX4 4QR
UK

www.exeterpress.co.uk

British Library Cataloguing in Publication Data
A catalogue record for this book is available
from the British Library.

Paperback ISBN 1-904675-03-4
Hardback ISBN 1-904675-40-9

Printed in Great Britain by
Antony Rowe Limited

*In loving memory of my mother Edith Metford,
linguist and teacher, on her birthday.*

19th June, 2003
Bristol

Contents

Preface

Opportunities to revisit a book come rarely, and I am most grateful to John Betts for providing one, even though the experience is salutary rather than reassuring. It is a special pleasure that Bristol Phoenix Press is producing the revised edition: long may this phoenix flourish! The first version followed the conventions of the *Landmarks in Classical Literature* series, edited by J.P. Stern; Cambridge University Press has kindly allowed reversion of rights. I have corrected some (doubtless not all) mistakes, changed my mind on some points, and tried to answer different questions from a different series editor. I hope the revised version has benefited from ten more years of reading Augustine whenever academic life allowed, but those years have made the conclusion to this book (*Confessions* 6.11.18) more deeply felt than ever. The purpose of the book remains unchanged: to encourage those who have not yet become readers of Augustine and especially of *Confessions*, and to be of some use to those who have. It is, as always, a pleasure to acknowledge a debt to the many scholars whose work has been a source of illumination.

* * * *

Augustine is one of the most influential writers of western culture, *Confessions* is the most read and discussed of all his many books, and there is an overwhelming bibliography on every one of them. What I have chiefly tried to do, in this short introductory book, is to set *Confessions* in the context of late antiquity. In the fourth and fifth centuries, the values of an inherited literary and philosophical culture were being challenged and a long-lasting political system was under threat. Western Europe was beginning to take shape as Roman political control declined and Christianity became the accepted faith. This social and intellectual context shaped what Augustine says about himself, God, language and narrative. Readers have understood *Confessions* in many ways, and Augustine himself, as a teacher of rhetoric and a gifted preacher, was particularly aware of different responses to written or spoken language. But there is a fundamental difference between this awareness of individual response and the critical theories that say there can be no authoritative reading of any text, or any canon of authoritative writings, because neither the author nor the expert (critic or historian) can determine how any individual actually reads texts. Augustine believes that there is an authoritative reading of his own and every life, known to God if not to him; that there is a canonical text, namely the Bible; and that there is a canon of interpretation, namely the fundamental Christian belief in love of God and love of neighbour. Multiple readings, of a text or a life, are equally valid – provided they are all in accord with this basic truth.

Chapter 1 uses recent work on social history and philosophy to interpret the world in which Augustine lived and the choices he made, in his education, his career, and his search for under-standing of himself and of God. Chapter 2 is concerned with the interpretation of a life, by the person who lives it and by others who accept or challenge that account. It deals both with literary questions about models and style and audience and with questions about what actually matters in a life. Translations of Augustine and other authors are my own, because I wanted to keep as close as possible to the original. More elegant translations of *Confessions* are listed in Further Reading (p. 97). Augustine uses the masculine when speaking of God, but, fortunately, addresses God as 'you' throughout *Confessions*; so I have not had to make the usual decision between masculine pronouns (for historical reasons) and inclusive language (for theological ones). For historical reasons, I have used the masculine in general references to fourth century professional speakers and bishops. All dates are CE unless it is otherwise stated. References to *Confessions* follow the convention of book number followed by both chapter and paragraph number: e.g. *C.* 10.18.27. Augustine divided his text into books, but the chapters and paragraphs are alternative later systems for subdividing it: chapters derive from the early printed

editions of the fifteenth and sixteenth century, paragraphs from
the seventeenth-century edition by the Benedictine monks of
St. Maur. So paragraphs run consecutively through a book, not
through a chapter.

Introduction

Take the books you wanted, my *Confessions*: look at me there so as not to praise me more than I am; believe what I say, not what others say, about me. Attend to me there and see what I was in myself and by myself. And if something in me pleases you, join me there in praising Him whom I wanted to be praised on my account - not me, for He made us, we did not make Him. [Augustine, *Letter* 231.6]

Augustine wrote this late in his life in response to a letter from an admirer, and it helps to explain the purpose of the *Confessions*, which he had written years before, at the end of the fourth century. The English word *'Confessions'* puts readers on the wrong track. It suggests the story of an exciting and sometimes wicked life, and that is the element of *Confessions* that attracts many readers: teenage gangs in Augustine's home town of Thagaste; disruptive students at Carthage; Augustine's sexual needs; his friend Alypius, who was taken to a gladiator show and became addicted to bloodshed. The text may sometimes encourage readers to expect such excitements; but the Latin word *confessio* means 'acknowledging' in a wider sense. Augustine wrote *Confessions* for people (some suspicious, some admiring) who wanted to know how a rising young teacher of Latin rhetoric had come to be what he then was – a bishop who lived in celibacy and austerity, a spiritual not a political leader. He had the double purpose of acknowledging his own weakness and acknowledging the power of God manifested in his own life and in all creation. It is in this sense that his book is a confession, of sin, of faith and of praise. One man's life becomes a way of demonstrating true religion. His experience also displays the transformation of Roman culture and, with it, the transformation of thinking about oneself.

Confessions is often, misleadingly, called 'the first auto-biography', the first narrative of an individual life. But how can anyone, with or without precedent, describe his or her own life?

What is to be selected or omitted, and how can the story be brought to an end when its subject goes on living? The point chosen as the conclusion, which 'closes' the narrative, determines the shape of the story. (Once 'Reader, I married him' was the closure of far too many stories about women.) Augustine seems to end his story in book nine, with his baptism as a Christian and the death of his mother who had constantly prayed for him; but then *Confessions* goes on. To present-day expectations, and probably to fourth-century expectations too, *Confessions* is a puzzling work. The problem can be described in Augustine's own words: when he re-read *Confessions* and all his other works in his last illness, he noted that books one to ten were about him, the other three about the creation narrative in the first verses of the Bible. He did not say why.

One provisional answer is that what interests him is the existence of a human being in relation to God the creator. If the question is 'Who am I?', Augustine is not satisfied with the answer 'son of Patricius and Monica of Thagaste in Africa, formed by such and such a family and education, friends and books and experience': he is a child of God, a prodigal son who squandered his inheritance, lived on food fit for pigs, and came back at last to his home. He begins the story of his own life with the infancy he cannot remember, because that is where 'I' begin, and he sees there the beginning of God's love and of human alienation from God. He selects events and stages of thought that map his journey away from home, away from God; and the beginning of his return. He ends the story of his life perhaps fifteen years before the time of writing *Confessions*, with his own rebirth as a baptised Christian and the death of his mother, who had been both a constant Christian presence and a tie to his former life.

Why, then, does the book not end where the life-story does? Again, a provisional answer is that what interests Augustine is the relationship between a human being and God. He reflects in book ten on what he has been doing in *Confessions* and asks how it has been possible for him to do it. How can the human mind recall the past, and how can he long for God without knowing God, who is beyond all human knowledge? He invokes God's help as he confesses not only his past errors, but also his present faith and his partial understanding of the theological problems that had kept him outside the church. The problem of evil was especially troubling; for, if God created the world and human kind, where did evil come from? In books eleven to thirteen Augustine interprets the first few verses of the Bible, using all the available techniques of multiple readings and hidden significance, to ensure that his readers get their theology right and do not, as he had done, think of God as good but powerless against evil, or as good and therefore remote from messy human existence.

The effect of *Confessions* altogether, Augustine said when he reread them, was to arouse the human mind and emotions towards God. They did it so well that, unlike most texts of European literature, they survived the age of manuscript in many copies. They have shaped and interpreted the experience of Christians from the time of writing until now. At the same time they also speak to readers who are not concerned with their lives, or with Augustine's, as focussed on God.

Confessions is sometimes called 'the first modern book'. As it happens, Augustine is one of the first Latin writers to use the adjective *modernus* – from Latin *modo* ('just now'). To call the *Confessions* 'modern' signals recognition of Augustine's awareness of himself and of multiple interpretations. What he says about himself is very different from earlier self-descriptions that survive from the Roman world, and often very close to the concerns of the present day. He describes emotionally charged relationships: with his mother, his friends, and above all with God. He combines vivid presentation and analysis with a sense that his own motives are beyond his intellectual reach: he is both fascinating and mysterious to himself, always dissatisfied with himself, and always aware of conflict and limitation. Books are as important as people in his life, and present-day readers recognise Augustine's awareness both of himself as reader and writer and of his audience as readers, how language affects him and them, how a life can in practice, not only in the writing of autobiography, be shaped by literary models. Augustine is sure that without language, his own or that of others, there is no memory: he cannot retain, or pass on to others, what he cannot put into words. But a life can be read differently at different times; by choosing different words and different literary models to convey what is happening to them, people reinterpret not only their memories, but also their present experience.

When Augustine first went to Carthage, aged seventeen, to begin his higher education, he tried out different interpretations of the longing and the dissatisfaction that he felt. There was sexual desire for a partner, a wish to be 'in love' as in Virgil's account of Carthaginian Dido's love for Aeneas, which he read as a schoolboy and now saw more crudely presented in performances at the theatre in Carthage. There was also the love of wisdom, philosophy, described in the (lost) *Hortensius* of Cicero. Augustine read it at just the right time in his life and later he would often suggest it to clever people in search of God, even though it is not a Christian text. The *Hortensius* inspired him to seek further wisdom and, since his mother had tried to bring him up a Christian, he turned to the Bible. But at that stage of his life the Bible was such unsatisfying reading that he did not interpret his longing as the desire for God.

Virgil and the Bible, the masterpiece of the Latin classical canon and the canon of authoritative Christian scripture, are the texts Augustine most often uses in the *Confessions* to interpret his life to himself. An image they have in common expresses these different desires:

> Sick with desire, and seeking him she loves,
> From street to street the raving Dido roves.
> So, when the watchful shepherd, from the blind,
> Wounds with a random shaft the careless hind,
> Distracted with her pain she flies the woods,
> Bounds o'er the lawn, and seeks the silent floods.
> [Virgil, *Aeneid* 4.68-73, in Dryden's adaptation]

> Like as the hart desireth the waterbrooks, so longeth
> my soul after thee, O God; my soul is athirst for God,
> yea, even for the living God.
> [*Psalm* 42, verses 1-2, as in the *Book of Common Prayer*
> 1662]

Did Virgil or the Bible offer the true description of Augustine's state of mind when he began his higher education at Carthage? The question is still in dispute. Some people agree with his own later diagnosis: that he failed to recognise his deepest desire for God because his head was full of popular romantic literature (*C.* 3.1.1-2). Others think that he projected on to God feelings of desire and guilt that were sexual in origin. It depends what they think themselves about what matters in a human life. What was really happening to Augustine? It depends how his – or anyone's – story ends; and no one knows that.

Part 1

Augustine's world

Africa: world politics

Augustine was a local boy who made good, a provincial from an upland farm in the Roman province of Africa. This meant North Africa (present-day Morocco, Algeria, Tunisia and Libya), on the southern edge of the Roman empire which, in the late fourth century, still extended from Spain to the Euphrates and from the Rhine to the Sudan. Rome had ruled this huge territory for over three hundred years, but at a high cost. There were endless wars, on the frontiers and between rival claimants to power. Roman citizens were heavily taxed to pay for the armies, which also requisitioned their food, transport and labour. Slavery was taken for granted and the supply of slaves was ensured by breeding, capture and kidnapping. Many people who were not actually slaves were legally bound to an inherited trade or piece of land, so that they could not move away from danger or poverty. Strong emperors, like Constantine (324-37) and Theodosius I (379-95), could hold the empire together, but the defence of most areas had to be left to powerful *duces* (Leaders) and *comites* (Companions of the Emperor), the forerunners of mediaeval dukes and counts. Such local leaders often decided that they could do better for themselves, and perhaps for their people, without imperial control. This happened in Africa twice during Augustine's lifetime. The result was war.

The empire, even when politically united, was not a religious or a cultural unity. Constantine ended the persecution of Christians and gave lavish support to Christian churches, but there were religious differences among Christians. As the fourth century progressed, the public practice of traditional Roman religion was

1

restricted, though many people continued to honour the gods of Rome. The eastern and western regions of the empire differed in language and in cultural patterns. The eastern empire – in Greece, Asia Minor and the Middle East – spoke Greek and looked to Constantine's new Christian capital, Constantinople, or to the ancient cities of Antioch and Alexandria. The western empire – Italy and France and Spain – spoke Latin and was beginning to look away from Rome, the source of its traditions and home of its aristocracy, to newer centres such as Milan and Trier, which were closer to the major routes of troop movements. Roman Africa belonged to the Latin west.

It is only a short sea crossing from the province of Africa to Sicily, Italy or Spain and, in Augustine's time, this link was more important than the journey eastwards to Greek-speaking Alexandria. The Arab conquest, which linked the North African coast to the Middle East as part of the Islamic world, came two centuries after his death. But Africa's connection with the Middle East was much older than that. The capital city of Roman Africa, Carthage, had originally been settled (in the eighth century BCE) by Phoenicians from the Middle East. Carthage and Rome had fought three devastating Punic Wars (Punic from *Poeni*, the Latin for Phoenicians) which ended with Roman conquest in the mid-second century BCE. Dialects of Punic were still spoken in country districts, and many people, including Augustine, understood a few words, though it was hard to find clergy who spoke anything other than Latin.

Augustine's mother Monica had a local, non-Roman, name but her culture, too, was Latin; he shows no awareness of himself as other than Roman, part of the dominant Mediterranean culture. It is sometimes suggested that, because he was African, he may have been black, and that he does not mention it because Romans took no particular notice of skin colour. Unfortunately, Romans did not lack colour prejudice, though it is quite true that they were just as rude about gangling red-haired Celts as they were about thick-lipped Ethiopians. The association of blackness and badness is all too evident in a fourth-century collection of stories about the 'Desert Fathers', the monks who lived in solitude or in community on uncultivated (Greek *eremos*, 'deserted') land in

Egypt. Father Moses was black and his bishop said at his ordination, 'Now you are all white'. 'But what am I inside?', Moses asked and, when his fellow clergy tested his humility by chasing out the 'black man', he reflected that they were right; for his skin was black as ashes. Augustine uses the association of black and bad just as unthinkingly, when he refers to 'the example of your servants whom you had made shining white from black, alive from dead' (*C.* 9.2.3). If he had been black, could he have resisted the rhetorical contrast between his skin colour and his redemption? 'African', for him, means someone who lives in North Africa and probably has the distinctive African accent. In his time Roman Africa looked north.

Danger to the Roman empire was also to come from the north. Central Asian tribes, moving (so far as anyone could see) quite unpredictably, displaced peoples whose names have become synonyms for ignorant destruction – Huns, Goths, Vandals. They moved across the Rhine and Danube into the empire, sometimes fighting against the armies of Rome and sometimes for them in return for land. When Augustine was in the early years of his teaching career (378) the Goths defeated the emperor Valens only a little way from Constantinople. Not quite ten years after he wrote *Confessions*, there was a mass movement of non-Romans across the Rhine and the Roman government pulled its troops out of Britain to meet the threat. The year after that (410) Alaric the Goth besieged and sacked Rome. Many people saw this disaster as the end of an era, the final retribution for neglecting the gods of Rome in favour of the Christian God.

Augustine did not see it like that. He knew his Roman history, an endless succession of wars and disasters survived; and, even if this was the end of Roman power in the west, he saw no reason to think that any one empire was of particular importance. His great work *City of God*, begun in response to the challenge of Roman refugees from the Gothic sack, contrasts the 'city of this world' with the heavenly city. The 'city of this world' is not the political regime that God has allowed to prevail for a time: it is the community made up of all those who love the fame, wealth, power and satisfaction that earthly life can provide. The citizens of the heavenly city, resident aliens in the place where they live, are all those who love God; and only God knows who is a citizen of which city.

Augustine did not live to see how the western empire, in the last decades of the fifth century, was replaced by kingdoms of Goths, Vandals, Franks and other 'barbarians' who still claimed some continuity with Roman tradition; or how the Christian church, simply by surviving, became the preserver of the Latin language and of Roman culture. In 429, the year before his death, the Vandals crossed from Spain to Africa, killing and plundering. He had been bishop of Hippo Regius (*hippo* is Punic for 'port', *regius* Latin for 'royal') for thirty-five years. The town was under siege when he died. Possidius, who wrote a brief biography of Augustine and a catalogue of his books, recorded some of his last words. They came from two texts that were so important in his life, and in *Confessions*, that they need preliminary explanation here. On the walls of Augustine's small room were texts of the seven penitential psalms. The Book of Psalms (also called the Psalter) in the Bible is a collection of songs addressed to God, and Augustine had chosen those that particularly express repentance for sin. He also quoted Plotinus, the third century CE Platonist philosopher, who was not a Christian, but whose work had helped Augustine, forty years earlier, to a better understanding of God. As the Vandals encircled his town, Augustine quoted 'The good man will not think it a great matter if sticks and stones fall and mortals die.'

Thagaste: family, church and school

In the small town of Thagaste in upland Numidia (now Souk Ahras in eastern Algeria), Augustine's childhood at least was safe from wars. He tells his readers (*C.* 2.3.5) that his father Patricius was not rich. He was not exactly poor either, since he was a *decurio*, a member of the local council of Thagaste – an honour most men tried to avoid, as decurions were responsible for shortfalls in the tax-collection and were expected to help out the local budget. Patricius, who was not a committed Christian, had a devout Christian wife, Monica. There were at least three children. Augustine was probably the eldest; he had a brother, who appears without explanation at the deathbed of their mother (*C.* 9.11.27), and a sister who never appears in *Confessions* but later became the leader of a community of Christian women. Sibling relationships do not feature in *Confessions*: it is his friends and his mother who matter to Augustine, because he could talk to them about religion.

Patricius could afford to send his clever son away to school in the nearby town of Madaura. Schooling was not cheap: parents negotiated with individual teachers, who expected presents as well as fees; and students needed an allowance. Then came a year which Augustine had to spend at home (*C.* 2.3.5), getting into bad company, while his father found the money for his higher education at Carthage, the capital city of Africa. Patricius could not have done it without help from Romanianus, a local landowner and benefactor, who continued to support Augustine in his later career. At Carthage, Augustine studied rhetoric and thought about religion. His mother had tried to bring him up a Christian, but he had not yet made a commitment to Christianity.

Roman Africa had a powerful tradition of martyrdom, religious conflict and public denunciation of sinners. It has been called the 'Bible belt' of the Roman empire. Bishops were expected to preach every Sunday, expounding the scriptures *ex cathedra*: *cathedra* is Latin for a high-backed chair, the sign of status which dominated the church building as a professor's chair dominated the lecture hall or a presiding official's the courtroom. So the cathedral church was the bishop's church. Many of the Christian laity came to church chiefly for the sermon, because, if they were not yet baptised, they did not stay for the Eucharist (communion). Baptism wiped out past sin, but many Christians did not see how they could be forgiven if they sinned after baptism. So they remained as catechumens (Christians under instruction) until they thought they could make the commitment. Patricius, Augustine's father, delayed baptism until late in life (*C.* 9.9.21). Augustine's mother made him a catechumen as a baby and he himself wanted to be baptised as a child when he was very ill. However, when he recovered, she deferred his baptism (*C.* 1.11.17) because of the risk of sin. He was still a churchgoer when he went to Carthage – indeed, he picked up a girlfriend in church (*C.* 3.3.5) – but he had not yet found any Christian preaching or writing suited to the intellectual level he needed.

There was such writing available but Augustine seems not to have known it when he was young. Africa had been Latin-speaking for at least three hundred years before his birth, with a local tradition of elaborate rhetoric and a reputation for producing lawyers. Tertullian in the second century and Cyprian in the third, both from Carthage, were brilliant examples both of Latin rhetoric and of African Christianity. In his life as a bishop Augustine found Cyprian especially helpful but as a young man he had not encountered good theological writing in Latin, and he thought the Latin Bible crude by comparison with the Virgil and Cicero he had read at school. This was a real barrier for educated Romans in the fourth century. In the early 380s, about the time when Augustine moved to Italy to teach, Bishop Damasus of Rome set Jerome on the task of producing a Latin Bible acceptable to the modern church. Jerome, like Augustine, was a brilliant young rhetorician. He came from northern Italy and was taught in Rome by the great Donatus, whose Latin grammar continued in use throughout the middle ages. The new translation later became known as the Vulgate, the 'commonly used' (Latin *vulgatus*) version. It did more than improve the Latin style; for Jerome went back to the Hebrew and Greek texts and did serious critical work on the tradition, with advice from Jewish scholars.

The new translation created new problems. When Augustine became a bishop, he used Jerome's translation of the Gospels in his church at Hippo; but he also wrote to Jerome to tell him how a local church had complained about the Old Testament. They had always heard that the prophet Jonah sat (improbably) under a gourd, whereas Jerome had him seated under ivy. Augustine thought this reaction revealed the more general problem that Jerome had undermined confidence in the Septuagint, the standard Greek translation of the Hebrew Old Testament. The Septuagint is so called because, according to legend, the seventy (Latin *sept-uaginta*) translators, each working in isolation, had been divinely inspired to produce identical versions. Augustine the intellectual could live with uncertainty, but Augustine the bishop knew the problems of those who could not.

Impressive theological writing was produced during Augustine's youth, especially by the three 'Cappadocian Fathers' from central Asia Minor: Basil, Gregory of Nazianzus and Gregory of Nyssa. It was inaccessible to him because it was in Greek. Many people along the North African coast spoke Greek, but Augustine had to learn it at school and found it hard going. Characteristically he ascribed his difficulties to sinful disobedience, not to bad teaching methods (*C.* 1.13.20.). Nor, evidently, were there any Christian intellectuals on hand in Thagaste and Madaura to inspire him. Augustine's mother, like most women of her time, had little education; she could only hope and pray and set an example, not argue with her brilliant son. So Augustine's adolescence was shaped by the great works of the classical literary tradition, above all the prose of Cicero and the poetry of Virgil.

Primary school taught basic literacy and numeracy to both boys and girls. Boys who went on to a *grammaticus* ('teacher of letters') expected to study a few classical authors, four or five hundred years old, chosen for style rather than content. Four authors were especially popular. Virgil (d. 19 BCE) was unquestionably the greatest Latin poet and Cicero (d. 43 BCE) the greatest writer of prose, both political oratory and philosophical discussion. The historian Sallust, a younger contemporary of Cicero, had a more 'pointed' style, and African schoolboys may have particularly liked his narrative of Rome's war with the Numidian prince Jugurtha. The dramatist Terence (d. 159 BCE), born in North Africa, wrote pure conversational Latin. These texts were read with very close attention to grammar and vocabulary, correctness of speech, choice and arrangement of words to evoke a specific response, cultural allusions – everything that would allow these schoolboys, in later life, to display their own culture. Little survives of 'vulgar Latin' (Latin in common use), because educated people were trained to use classical Latin for any public purpose and it is their writings that were copied. The gap between the literary classics and everyday Latin may have been rather like the gap between Shakespeare and the speech of present-day schoolchildren, though there is an important difference: past generations of schoolchildren grew up reading and quoting Shakespeare but were not trained to write like him. The *grammaticus* had to spend time teaching his pupils how to read a text written without word-divisions or systematic punctuation, and in a form of Latin unlike that which they actually spoke. It was all reinforced with beatings (*C.* 1.9.14), like a caricature of an old-style English public school. Nevertheless, Augustine learned to love Virgil.

Every schoolboy knew the *Aeneid,* the great epic poem, written almost four hundred years earlier, which had both a literary and a political programme. Virgil had set out to show that Latin poetry could rival Homer and the Greeks; and that Roman imperial rule was ordained by the gods and destined to endure. His hero Aeneas experiences both the fighting of Homer's *Iliad* and the search for home of Homer's *Odyssey*; yet the defining characteristic of Aeneas is not the fighting skills of Achilles or the survival skills of Odysseus, but *pietas*, a characteristically Roman devotion to family, duty and the will of the gods. The *Aeneid* continued to be the charter-text of Roman education, even when Christian emperors ruled and the worship of Virgil's gods was actively discouraged. When Augustine was a small boy, Julian 'the apostate' (361-3), the only emperor after Constantine to renounce Christianity, said that Christians should not hold teaching posts unless they could accept the religious values of the classical literature they taught. Some Christians, including Augustine and Jerome, expressed anxiety about the influence of that literature on impressionable children. But the classical curriculum survived.

Augustine, like most young students of Virgil, was less impressed by the grandeur of Roman destiny than by the story of Dido queen of Carthage. Dido's love for Aeneas almost diverts him from his destined task of founding Rome; it destroys her and puts her people at risk. Virgil gives more persuasive voices to the rage and suffering of Rome's (usually female) victims than he does to his Roman hero. Aeneas is obedient to destiny (Latin *fatum*), which is voiced by Jupiter, father of gods and men. He leaves his ruined city carrying his aged father and leading his young son, a living image of Roman patriarchy, losing his wife Creusa whom he has told to follow at a distance. Destiny forbids him to become the consort of Dido, a refugee like himself, who is building the city of Carthage for her people. She sees their relationship as marriage; he does not. He is distressed by their parting; she commits suicide. This is, of course, a present-day reading of Virgil. Augustine, a man of the fourth century, accepts patriarchy as part of the natural order. Yet he took from Virgil – and uses in the *Confessions* – images of destructive love, anguished parting and the journey of an often bewildered man who seeks to interpret the Father's command.

Carthage: rhetoric and religion

Virgil was also a path to success. The schoolboy Augustine won high praise for composing and delivering a (prose) speech in which Juno, queen of the gods, rages at her inability to keep Aeneas out of Italy. Looking back, he saw it as dust and ashes (*C*. 1.12.21): a false god, false emotions, praise for a meaningless achievement; but further education in rhetoric, expensively bought at Carthage, was his family's investment for the future. The most obvious route into the imperial civil service (*militia civilis*) was to be an advocate or a legal adviser on the staff of the provincial governor, whose time was mostly taken up with lawsuits.

Augustine was now learning the 'liberal arts', literally the skills suitable for a free man. 'Free' in this context does not mean 'as opposed to slave'; for both slaves and hired professionals depended for their living on the orders of someone else. The 'liberal arts' were for people who were free to study what they found interesting. If such a 'free man' wanted to study medicine or architecture or engineering, he did it as a form of philosophy, aiming to understand the workings of the physical world or the human body, not because he needed to market his technical skills. 'Natural philosophy' survived into the nineteenth century as a name for what is now called science. (It is another question why, in English, that particular study should appropriate the Latin word for 'knowledge', *scientia*.)

At school Augustine had studied grammar (the correct use of language) and begun rhetoric. He now added dialectic (the techniques of analysis and argument). This included the study of Aristotle's *Categories*, a text that many students found difficult. He thought it quite straightforward and could not see why his tutor was so excited about it (*C*. 4.16.28). More abstract analysis led to arithmetic and geometry and their applications in music and astronomy. Augustine's African contemporary Martianus Capella named these disciplines 'the seven liberal arts'; and they became the *trivium* (three roads meeting: grammar, rhetoric, dialectic) and the *quadrivium* (four roads meeting: arithmetic, geometry, astronomy, music), a curriculum inherited by mediaeval universities. Even a liberal education had a practical aim. Roman education was intended to produce expert speakers, just as present-day education in 'the arts' has, until very recently, aimed to produce expert writers. Rhetoric was the ability to make language do justice to the horror or glory of what was happening; and to inspire and persuade an audience both by appropriate speech and by the right kind of argument. Successful rhetoric required acute awareness of how language is used and how people respond. Education trained students in the exact sense of words and the organisation of a speech. It provided a repertory of argument, example and cultural allusion. The study of rhetoric included memory training and body-language: gesture, eye-contact, breath-control, pitch and cadence of voice.

Augustine needed to make a career and his family had planned (*C*. 3.3.6) that he should be a lawyer. Instead, he became a teacher of rhetoric, a profession that could also lead into the civil service. At the time when he decided to abandon his pursuit of success, ten years after he finished his own education, his teaching career had taken him from home to Carthage, then to Rome and finally to be the publicly funded teacher of rhetoric at Milan, making speeches before the imperial court.

Augustine did not only want success: he wanted to lead a morally good life. One of his set books at Carthage (*C*. 3.4.7) was the *Hortensius* of Cicero. Although he began to read it with an eye to style, it was the content that impressed him. The *Hortensius* now survives only in quotations, many of them by Augustine himself, but there is no doubt that its explicit purpose was to encourage the study of philosophy. Philosophy (literally, the love of wisdom) meant, for almost every Greek or Roman philosopher since Plato, the desire to understand the gods' (or God's) design for the universe and for the human soul. It required not only intellectual effort but invocation and contemplation of the divine, along with a disciplined life that avoided distractions. This disciplined life was called *askesis* (Greek 'training', as for a race – hence 'ascetic'). But there are many kinds of asceticism. In Augustine's time, some Christian ascetics went in for extremes of self-deprivation, even self-torment, and several Christian writers, especially Jerome, proclaimed the virtues of men and women who renounced family duties and worldly wealth. Non-Christian philosophers were wary of greed, lust and ambition, but usually combined the love of wisdom with traditional family and civic obligations.

Plato and the philosophers who followed him directed attention away from this changeable world to the absolute good which, they believed, can be grasped by the exercise of reason. Human beings, they argued, are distinctively rational animals and reason, which allows us to make sense of the world, is the aspect of humans which is closest to the divine. So intellectual work and prayer are not separate activities. The more someone loves wisdom, the more they become like God, and they may eventually attain union with God in that their thoughts will not be other than God's thoughts. But the further someone is from God, the more fragmented they become, because their attention is dispersed over the multiplicity and un-reality of this world, not focussed on God. Greed for pleasure or power, anger, sexual passion, are all distractions from what people ought to be doing. So the decision to follow philosophy could amount to conversion, a radical change of lifestyle in favour of simplicity and study.

Augustine read the *Hortensius* at just the right age and remembered it all his life. He was a Christian catechumen; so, perhaps for the first time, he started to read the Bible for guidance on how he should live. He found not only the style, but also the content, disconcerting. If God made all that there is, did God make evil too? If God said, 'Let us make man in our image', does that imply that God is like a human being? Are we really supposed to admire the patriarchs of Israel? 'Where does evil come from, and is God confined within a bodily form, and does God have hair and nails, and can men be called righteous when they have several wives at once, kill people and sacrifice animals?' (*C*. 3.7.12).

These questions were asked by missionaries of the Manichaean religion, which Augustine followed for the next nine years (*C.* 4.1.4). Until quite recently, Manichaeism was known only from Christian polemic, much of it written by Augustine in his later career, and it was difficult to see what could have been the attraction for intelligent people. But the discovery of Manichaean texts has made it clearer. Mani, the founder of Manichaeism, came from southern Mesopotamia, a meeting-point of religious traditions, and probably belonged to an austere Judaeo-Christian sect. He left it in the late 230s, believing that he had received a revelation, and he presented his revelation in a form that could spread east and west, adapting to local religions: some surviving Manichaean texts come from Turfan in China; and a Manichaean psalm-book from the early centuries CE was found at Nag Hammadi in Egypt. There was an elaborate mythology of angelic and demonic powers that explained the workings of the universe; it could be understood as a 'story' version of philosophical theories on the different levels of being which are intermediate between the physical world and the divine One. Mani acknowledged Jesus as a divine being, but this entailed rejecting much of the New Testament as a false record (*C.* 5.11.21). He also rejected the Biblical account of creation. The book of Genesis declares that the universe is God's creation: 'and God saw that it was good'. Mani taught that the physical world is temporary and deceptive. Light (the power of good) has been invaded by darkness (the power of evil) and is now dispersed and entrapped in matter. Everything that happens in the material world – and in an individual life – can be explained as an aspect of the struggle between light and darkness. The hope of those who have seen the light is to be freed from their lower (physical) nature, which keeps them in this world.

'Manichaean' still means an insistence on seeing things in stark oppositions of right and wrong. For Christians, a 'Manichaean' attitude means refusal to accept that human bodily existence, even though flawed by sin, is God's good creation. Manichaean leaders, the Elect Saints, were celibate and taught their disciples to avoid procreation. The Elect were also strict vegetarians, because they were forbidden to take any life, even that of a plant. In his polemic against Manichaeism Augustine found diet a rich theme for mockery. The digestive system of the Elect could liberate, by burping or retching (*C.* 3.10.18), particles of light trapped in the food. (Melons and cucumbers had a particularly high light content.) The Elect had to eat something; so their disciples incurred the guilt of preparing the food and the Elect prayed for them. It is possible to invent a more sympathetic explanation. Food is a mark of mortality, because the human body needs constant refuelling. Mani perhaps taught that even the processes of digestion and excretion could contribute to the liberation of the divine from the material world. When he wrote *Confessions,* Augustine was still suspected of Manichaean tendencies and this is one reason why he insists (*C.* 10.31.46) that he is not worried about eating impure food.

Food provides Augustine with one of the dominant images of *Confessions* 3 and 4. He compares the inadequate spiritual food supplied by Manichaeism, as well as the fictions of classical literature, to the 'husks that the swine did eat', the garbage that the Prodigal Son was reduced to eating when he left his father's house and wasted his inheritance. The story of the Prodigal Son (told in the gospel according to Luke) is one of Jesus' parables, stories with a meaning for those who can hear it. It was especially important to Augustine and deserves retelling for itself.

A man had two sons. The younger said to his father, 'Father, give me my share of the property'. And he divided his livelihood between them. Soon afterwards the younger son put all his share together and went abroad into a far country, where he lived a dissolute life and squandered his property. When he had spent it all there was a severe famine in that country, and he began to be in want. He attached himself to one of the citizens of the country, who sent him to his estate to feed the pigs. He wanted to fill himself with the husks that the pigs ate, and no one gave him anything. Then he came to himself and said, 'How many of my father's hired hands have more bread than they can eat, while I am dying of hunger? I will get up and go to my father, and say to him, "Father, I have sinned against heaven and in your eyes, and I do not deserve to be called your son; treat me as

one of your hired hands"'. So he got up and went to his
father. But while he was still far off his father saw him
and was deeply moved: he ran and clasped him in his
arms and kissed him. The son said, 'Father, I have sinned
against heaven and in your eyes, and I do not deserve to
be called your son'. But the father said to his servants,
'Quick, bring the best robe and put it on him, and a ring
for his finger and shoes for his feet, and bring the fatted
calf for us to have a feast. For this son of mine was dead
and has come back to life; he was lost and is found'.

(Luke 15.11-24).

In Carthage, teaching his students, Augustine was remote from
God: 'I was far away from you in a foreign country, shut out even
from the husks of the pigs whom I was feeding on husks' (*C.*
3.6.11). He was not one of the Manichaean Elect but a 'hearer', a
familiar term for the less committed students of a religious leader.
Like Christian catechumens, they received instruction. They
were not required to be celibate but were told to remain faithful
to one partner and to avoid procreation, since that would entrap
more spirits in matter. Augustine's concern in *Confessions* is to
acknowledge the ignorance and error of his time as a Manichaean,
not to explain why he became one. The answer to that question
may be that Manichaeism offered explanation, community and
demanding standards of conduct. It could assure Augustine that
behaviour he disliked in himself was caused by evil influences
outside his true self (*C.* 5.10.18), and it offered a solution to the
problem of where that evil came from. The 'problem of evil' is
that an omnipotent God has to be responsible for evil, either
by having brought it into being or by allowing it to continue. If
God is love, He would do neither. Mani's solution was to give
up omnipotence. If evil is an independent force, which can be
resisted but not overcome by good, then God is not to be blamed
either for creating evil or for allowing evil to continue.

Manichaeism had other attractions for Augustine besides
those of doctrine. Its texts were imposing, beautifully written and
decorated, and full of the 'true wisdom' in suitably mysterious
form. They were far more impressive than the Latin Bible, which

they encouraged Augustine to dismiss. There was also a strong Manichaean network, hidden from all but the true believers. Manichaeism was politically suspect, as any secretive association might be, but especially because it came from Mesopotamia and therefore might be a fifth column of Rome's major enemy, the Sassanid Persian empire. In fact the Sassanids also persecuted Manichaeans and Mani himself had died as a result of torture; but about that the Roman authorities either did not know or did not care. At the end of the third century, the emperor Diocletian ordered Manichaean books to be burned together with the Elect who possessed them. Augustine does not suggest that the Manichaeans he knew were actually in danger, but perhaps (as with Communist cells in the 1950s) they felt the excitement of being on the edge of danger while in the secret of the movement and the truth.

Gradually Augustine discovered that the Manichaeans of Carthage were not as profound as he had thought. When he asked a difficult question, they resorted to myths and metaphors; they assured him that everything would be explained when the great Faustus came. The Manichaean hierarchy was, deliberately, similar to the Christian, and Faustus was their bishop of Rome. Eventually, when Augustine was twenty-nine, Faustus did come to Carthage. He proved charming but a disappointment (C. 5.6.10-7.12). He was not nearly as well read as Augustine in the liberal arts: in particular, he was not good at astrology. Augustine had been reading widely in natural philosophy. He could not see how to reconcile the calculations of astronomers with Manichaean stories about the workings of the sun, moon and stars. Faustus admitted that neither could he. This problem had practical implications, because Augustine was, like many men of his time, very interested in astrology. It seemed obvious that the stars belonged to a higher and more ordered level of being than that of earthly life; plausible, too, that they had some influence on events in the world below them. So horoscopes could be properly scientific predictions in a dangerous world; and astrology could shift the blame for wrongdoing away from the individual and on to cosmic powers: 'Venus or Saturn or Mars did it' (C. 4.3.4).

Astrologers were called *mathematici*, a name that shows their reputation for abstruse knowledge and calculation. They could make a living from their skill – but at some risk: any enquiry that seemed political could lead to a charge of treason, with the threat of torture even for people of high social status. The fourth-century astrologer Firmicus Maternus tried to avoid this problem by declaring that it is impossible to ask about the emperor, because he is not subject to the decrees of Fate. At Carthage, Augustine had a distinguished friend, Vindicianus, who had studied astrology as a profession until he decided it was a bogus science and transferred to medicine (*C.* 4.3.5) It was some years later – he does not say exactly when – that Augustine finally lost confidence in astrology. His friend Firminius (*C.* 7.6.8) had been born at exactly the same time as a slave child in a nearby house. His father and the slave's owner were so interested in astrology that they cast horoscopes even for domestic animals. The two children had identical horoscopes: but their lives were as different as might be expected for the son of the house and a slave.

Africa to Italy: Manichaeans and pagans

Augustine says he was already dissatisfied with Manichaean mythology when he moved on from Carthage to Rome. In *Confessions* his mother's grief dominates the account of his departure. Gradual detachment from Manichaeism dominates his brief account of the months he spent in Rome. His silence about Rome itself is a puzzle. This was the ancient capital of empire, the place where Cicero delivered his speeches and Virgil gave readings of his epic, the ultimate purpose of Aeneas' journey from Carthage. It was also the place where the two greatest Christian apostles, Peter and Paul, were thought to have died as martyrs. Augustine arrived there in 383/4, a particularly interesting year in the relationship between Christianity and traditional Roman religion. In that year the influential bishop Damasus died. For almost twenty years he had raised funds for churches and martyr-shrines with elegant inscriptions to commemorate Rome's Christian heritage; and his personal status prompted a comment from a leading non-Christian: 'make me bishop of Rome and I'll be a Christian tomorrow!' It was in 383/4 too that the influential aristocrat Symmachus became Prefect of the City. He campaigned for the restoration of funding to traditional religion and symbolised his commitment to it by restoring the Altar of Victory to the Senate House. This altar became the focus of conflict between Symmachus and Ambrose, bishop of Milan, a former governor of his region who knew just how to apply political pressure.

Ambrose wanted the altar removed because it honoured a false god and was therefore unacceptable to a Christian emperor. Symmachus wanted it replaced because it expressed the traditional piety that had made Rome great. He argued that a Christian emperor need not reject it, because there are many ways of acknowledging the divine power that rules the universe. This dispute exemplifies two ways of understanding Roman religion. Christians called followers of the traditional religion 'pagans', which may be an army term for the 'civvies' who did not serve in the army of Christ or may mean 'hicks', because country people were thought to be ignorant. Yet there were many intelligent and high-minded pagans who believed in a single divine power, as advocated by Plato, but accepted the ancient rites as an important aspect of social cohesion and as recognition of the many ways in which God's power is evident in the world.

Augustine does not discuss Roman religion in *Confessions*, apart from a few dismissive comments (e.g. *C*. 8.2.3), because it is not part of his own intellectual history. He says very little about his time in Rome, either in *Confessions* or in his other works. Hostile ancient critics suggested that he had left Carthage one jump ahead of arrest as a Manichaean; some modern critics suggest that he edited out his time in Rome, deliberately or unconsciously, because it was not a success. Augustine says that his friends encouraged him to go to Rome for higher fees and greater status, but (like all good academics) he was interested only in having good students (*C*. 5.8.14) instead of the disruptive students of Carthage. In Rome he stayed at the house of another Manichaean 'hearer' but he was beginning to think (*C*. 5.10.19) that the Academic philosophers, whose arguments he knew from reading Cicero, were right to say that there is no conclusive proof of anything. He did not turn to the Christian church because he was still convinced by Manichaean rejection of the Old – and much of the New – Testament. He still thought (*C*.5.10.19-20) that Christians held a crudely anthropomorphic belief about God. He could imagine Christ emerging from the luminous body of God but did not see how Christ could be born of Mary without being contaminated by flesh. Nor did he have an answer to the devastating anti-Manichaean argument of his friend Nebridius, which he reports later in *Confessions* (*C*. 7.2.3). Mani taught that evil invaded good and dispersed good in fragments that are trapped in the material world. Nebridius asked what would happen if good (i.e. God) did not bother to fight back. If evil could damage God, then what kind of help can this damaged God give to the human souls that are enslaved in the material world? If evil could not damage God, what is the point of the great Manichaean struggle?

But in Rome Augustine was still associated with Manichaeans and this connection helped him to be considered for a publicly funded post at Milan (*C*. 5.13.23). Symmachus, himself a noted orator, had been asked to make the appointment; he may have been pleased to appoint a competent non-Christian to a post that required public speeches.

Milan: worldly success and renunciation

Augustine says that each move in his teaching career had some immediate emotional or practical motive. He taught for a time at Thagaste, his home town, but it became unbearable after the death of a friend (*C*. 4.7.12). The students at Carthage were disruptive (*C*. 5.8.14); and the students at Rome, though better behaved, cheated their teachers out of fees (*C*. 5.12.22). Each move was also a step up the ladder, from small town to provincial capital, then to the heart of empire. Rome was the ancient centre of empire and culture but Milan was now the emperor's Italian base: it was nearer the major army routes from France to the Balkans and better placed to respond to the endless movements of the northern tribes. Augustine's duties included panegyrics (*C*. 6.6.9), formal and (he says) quite untrue speeches of praise which advertised the achievements and intentions of the emperor. This was a particularly challenging task; for the western emperor, Valentinian II, was then aged only thirteen. Augustine might reasonably hope (*C.* 6.11.19) to end as governor of at least a minor province, if he married a wife with money and made good use of his contacts; he was not likely to be sent back to Africa, for its importance as a supplier of grain required a senior man. This may seem an odd way to choose a provincial governor, though it is no odder than the choice of administrators for large areas of the British empire in the nineteenth and early twentieth centuries. Many were young men who had demonstrated their ability, within the current educational system, by their command of Demosthenes and Cicero and their facility in writing Greek and Latin prose and verse. In the later Roman empire a teacher of rhetoric who became a governor would at least be able to make an effective speech or to write a persuasive report.

In the late fourth century the most high-minded public servants needed convincing that they ought to stay in their jobs. Ever since the days of Plato and Socrates, it had been argued that the cares of household management and government obstructed the pursuit of wisdom; but that the 'wise man' would do his duty to his family and his city. Christians were unconvinced: the New Testament encouraged them to think of fellow-Christians as their true family, themselves as citizens of another country, temporary residents in a world which could not last. This attitude did not present a problem while Christianity was a minority religion. But Constantine, only thirty years before Augustine's birth, had made Christianity an officially approved religion of the empire, and had given lavish subsidies to churches. Theodosius I, who became emperor when Augustine was twenty-five, put increasing pressure on those who tried to maintain the old religion. In practice he appointed the most suitable men he could find, regardless of their religious beliefs, but there were many Christians who held important posts.

The main functions of Roman imperial government were defence and law enforcement. Most governors had the 'right of the sword' (*ius gladii*), the authority to order execution. Yet Christians accepted the commandment 'Thou shalt not kill', together with Jesus' teaching that they must turn the other cheek. Not only were they instructed to refrain from murder, they should also meet violence with non-violence. How then could they be soldiers or give soldiers the order to kill or enforce the law by its usual methods of investigative torture, physical punishment for those who had nothing else to lose, and execution, sometimes carried out with extreme cruelty? Christian tradition had been formed in three centuries when there were always other people to serve in the army and exercise justice. It was extremely difficult to reconcile Christian pacifist teachings with the state's requirements of law and defence. Some Christians have always said it is impossible.

High-minded Romans, both Christian and non-Christian, tried to keep judicial violence to the minimum; but it was part of the system. According to his biographer, Ambrose, bishop of Milan, did not use judicial torture when he was a governor in northern Italy, until the moment when he ordered a suspect to be tortured in order to demonstrate to the people of Milan that Ambrose the governor was not a suitable choice as their bishop. Augustine's own commitment to Christianity came when he was perhaps a few years away from becoming governor of a province, with the authority to order criminals to be tortured and executed, and necessary involvement, even in the civil service, in financing and supplying the troops.

The use of force was not the only problem for people who wanted to lead good lives. Augustine brought friends with him to Milan (*C.* 8.6.13), young professional men like him, fellow-Africans trying to establish themselves in metropolitan careers and wondering if they were doing the right thing. Alypius was a lawyer, unemployed after three terms as a legal assessor 'selling advice'. Augustine himself was a 'word-salesman' (*C.* 9.5.13), a professional speaker and teacher, though he was not even sure that rhetoric can be taught. Nebridius was teaching literature as assistant to another friend. They were all engaged in perpetuating a system and a culture about which they had serious doubts; so they spent all the time they could in reading and discussing philosophy and theology. They were on the fringes of the Church: some of their best friends were Christians; so were some of the men they most admired. One of these was Ambrose.

Bishop Ambrose of Milan was a Roman aristocrat, trained in philosophy and rhetoric. He had been kind to Augustine on his arrival (*C.* 5.13.23). Augustine went to hear him preach, interested at first only by his rhetorical skill but coming to realise (*C.* 5.14.24-5) that Ambrose could interpret even the most off-putting sections of the Old Testament to show their spiritual value. Ambrose did this by using the technique employed by his 'pagan' opponents to interpret traditional rituals and mythology. He treated Scripture as allegory, a system of coded references to profound truths about God and the universe. He often cited the words of St Paul: 'the letter kills, but the spirit gives life' (*C.* 6.4.5). Paul meant the 'letter of the law', the written rules of the old agreement between God and his people, that 'kills' because inevitable disobedience leads to inevitable death. Ambrose, like many other Christian interpreters of the Bible, applied Paul's saying to the literal reading of texts. Just as strict observation of rules, and strict imposition of penalties for breaking them, can go against justice, so strict attention to the literal meaning of texts can go against truth.

Augustine may have heard Ambrose preach a series of sermons on the Six Days of Creation (*Hexaemeron*) in the first chapter of Genesis. On the sixth day God said, 'Let us make man in our image'; Ambrose challenged the literal Manichaean interpretation. If man is made in the image of God, Christians (according to the Manichaeans) must believe that God looks just like a human being. Ambrose drew on the tradition of Platonist philosophy to argue that it is the rational human soul, not the human body with its physical senses and passions, that is in God's image. It was the first time Augustine had heard Christianity expounded at this intellectual level. The Manichaean arguments against Christianity now looked as unconvincing as other parts of their teaching and Augustine decided that he could no longer be a member of the sect. His mother had come to join him at Milan and her devotion encouraged his interest in Christian practice. He went regularly with her to hear Ambrose preach. But he could not yet declare himself a committed Christian: his real concern was for the philosophy that Ambrose used so effectively in his sermons.

In Milan there was a group of intellectuals who met to study Platonist philosophy. One of them gave Augustine 'Platonist books' in Latin translation (*C.* 7.9.13). He does not say what exactly these books were. Many philosophers in late antiquity worked by debating the correct interpretation of Plato. They are often called 'neoplatonists'; but they did not think they were doing anything 'new'. They wanted to expound the implications of Plato's philosophy, just as Christian theologians wanted to expound the implications of Scripture. The 'Platonist books' probably included some works by the third century philosopher Plotinus, who taught in Rome, and perhaps some by his student Porphyry, who organised the unsystematic treatises of Plotinus into *Enneads* (groups of nine). Augustine is interested in telling readers about the arguments, rather than the authors. He had not wanted to think of God in human form but he did not know how to think of God, except in images of something physical that occupies space. Platonist texts directed his attention to the great power of the mind that forms these images but does not itself occupy space (*C.* 7.1.1-2). He was still preoccupied by the origin of evil: the Platonist texts argued that there is no independent power of evil. Corruption can only make sense (*C.* 7.12.18) if it is the corruption of something originally good, which has turned or fallen away from God. Everything owes its existence to God; so something that is utterly corrupt ceases to exist. It follows from this argument that apparent evils are really conflicts of interest (as in the case of humans and mosquitoes) or part of the workings of the universe (like floods and volcanic eruptions) or the consequence of bad choices.

Yet why should anything turn or fall away from God? Plotinus considered the possibility that it is by a free choice, a kind of self-assertiveness, but he was more interested in the route back. According to Platonist teaching, people must aim for becoming like God. Those who find themselves in the 'region of unlikeness' (*C.* 7.10.16) can climb back to higher things by the ascent of reason. This means that we must 'go into ourselves', reflect on our own thinking and how we make sense of the world, and understand what must be true for this activity to be possible. Eventually we may attain union with God, in that our thoughts will (for a moment) be the same as the thoughts of God, not multiple and successive as they usually are. Though Augustine tried to do what Plotinus taught, to 'lift the mind's eye' up to God (*C.* 7.3.5), he always fell back. 'I could not stand firm to enjoy my God, but I was caught up to you by your beauty and soon wrenched away from you by my weight and crashed groaning down into lesser things; and that weight was my carnal habit' (*C.* 7.17.23).

There was another choice to be made in the pursuit of wisdom. Augustine and his friends were uncertain whether they should continue their careers or devote their lives to study and prayer (*C.* 6.14.24). If they married, they would have a household and children to support. Their wives might reasonably object (*C.* 9.3.5) to their renouncing worldly concerns. If they did not marry, both Christians and non-Christian philosophers taught that they should live in chastity; for the only proper use of sex is within marriage for the procreation of children. Any other use is lust, which damages the soul.

Augustine had been living with a woman since he was a student at Carthage (*C.* 4.2.2). As a Manichaean 'hearer' he tried to avoid procreation. Nevertheless, they had a son, Adeodatus (the name means 'God's gift'), an unplanned yet much loved child. But Augustine's future career depended on finding a wife of good family with money of her own. His mother was negotiating a suitable marriage and that required him to send away his long-term partner. He found it impossible to manage without a temporary substitute, whose attraction was not long-standing affection but sex. Chastity, he thought, was beyond him. Meanwhile, he found his job stressful. He makes a rather trite contrast (*C.* 6.6.9) with the immediate happiness of a drunken beggar, but improves on it by suggesting that he was in a state of permanent, if depressed, intoxication by worldly fame. He was also confronted by examples of people who had achieved what he could not in philosophy.

Porphyry's biography of Plotinus described a man who 'seemed ashamed of being in a body' and who (like Porphyry himself on one occasion) had several times reached the height of contemplation, the point at which his thoughts were not distinct from the thoughts of God. Augustine could not reach this height by his own moral and intellectual effort and had not yet understood how Jesus Christ could mediate between God and human (*C.* 7.19.25). He 'seized on' the letters of St Paul (*C.*7.21.27) as a corrective to the Platonist books. Paul insisted that people must acknowledge their sinfulness and that only God's free gift can liberate them from the compulsion to sin. Christians call this gift 'grace' (Latin *gratia*, 'favour'). By contrast, non-Christian philosophers seemed to rely too arrogantly, or too optimistically, on human reason as a route to God. Augustine says he can remember (*C.* 7.20.26) the impact the Platonist books made on him before he read the Scriptures; he thinks it was meant that he should read them in that order, so that he could see the difference 'between presumption and confession'.

The difference is illustrated by the story Augustine told in book 6 of *Confessions* about his friend Alypius, who, although frankly puzzled by Augustine's enjoyment of sex (*C.* 6.12.21), had a comparable problem. Alypius was addicted to violence – not to inflict it himself but to see it inflicted at 'the games'. Roman games included fights to the death between men and animals (the more savage and exotic, the more popular) or between trained fighters. Intelligent Romans found enjoyment of them as repellent as an addiction to snuff movies. The emperor Constantine banned gladiator fights but it took another two centuries for the ban to be properly enforced. Alypius managed to break the habit when he was a student at Carthage only to succumb again at Rome when some friends dragged him along to a gladiatorial show. He told them they could take him but not make him watch (*C.* 6.8.13). He sat with his eyes shut; but he did not stop his ears and a roar from the crowd made him open them. One look was enough: he was addicted again, despite all his principles, until 'much later' God rescued him.

Reason had not been enough for Alypius or for Augustine. St. Paul thought that moral law was actually counter-productive, making people more aware of what was forbidden and more eager to do it (Romans 7.7-8). By the time Augustine wrote *Confessions* he had decided that the solution is not to oppose reason and desire – 'I want to do this, but I ought not to' – rather to acknowledge the deepest desire, which is for God. The love of God can overcome lesser loves: 'I want to do this, but there is something I want more'. It becomes possible, as he put it in his *Treatises on John's Gospel*, to 'love, and do what you will' (one of his most misunderstood sayings). The weight of sexual desire had pulled

Augustine down from the heights of contemplation; it became (*C.* 13.9.10) the weight of love that pulled him into his proper place, like a body settling to rest. Looking back on his time at Milan, he was chiefly aware of compulsion and frustration, the gulf between his human nature and God.

Platonist philosophers argued that God's unchanging love permeates and orders the universe and inspires those who achieve the higher levels of contemplation (*C.* 7.9.13); they did not offer Christ as the mediator between human nature and God. Many readers of *Confessions* wonder why Augustine does not say more about his study of the distinctive Christian doctrine of incarnation. Perhaps it would have been impossible to discuss it without writing several more books; or perhaps the fact was that he had not realised, at the time of his baptism, the nature of the problem. In 325 the church council of Nicaea, convened by the emperor Constantine, had offered a statement of belief on the relationship of Jesus Christ to the God whom he called Father. It was intended to be authoritative and eventually came to be so but, in the later fourth century, many people did not even know what it said; and those who did were still debating it. Theologians had not achieved a definition of how Christ could be fully God and fully human. Ambrose was engaged in a political conflict with 'Arian' Christians (*C.* 9.7.16): they accepted the theology of Arius, who was denounced (perhaps mistakenly) at Nicaea for teaching that Christ was superior to all created beings but subordinate to God. When Augustine and Alypius were in Milan, Alypius thought (*C.* 7.19.25) the official doctrine was that Christ was 'only God and flesh', without a human mind; and Augustine thought that Christ was a fully human being, one of exceptional wisdom, who experienced human temporal existence (at one time he is doing this, at another something else) and human suffering (physical pain, grief, fear, death). But Augustine wanted (*C.* 7.3.4) a God who is not subject to change or to corruption.

Plato argued that God is perfect goodness and therefore not subject to change, because any change would have to be for the worse. It followed that God could not have emotions, both because emotions require change from one kind of feeling to another and because emotion implied vulnerability. The Greek word *pathos* means emotion, but also experience, suffering, illness. Emotions, as it were, come from outside and attack people, who may succumb. So there was a problem about God in the Bible manifesting anger; for the anger meant that someone's wrongdoing had, so to speak, got to God. If God decided to spare a condemned city, did that mean that God had been wrong to condemn it? There was also a problem about Christ experiencing fear in the garden of Gethsemane and, worst of all, death on the cross. It seemed that what has to be true of a human being – genuine uncertainty, suffering, death – cannot also be true of God. How could a Platonist accept the incarnation?

But the problem that looms largest in *Confessions* is creation. The very first words of the Bible are: 'In the beginning God created the heavens and the earth'. In the philosophical tradition, the One God was not involved with the material universe: a lesser divine being, as in Plato's *Timaeus*, did the work of creation. And how could there be such a beginning? Genesis seems to suggest that God decided, at a particular moment in time, to create the universe. If so, had God allowed a less good state of affairs to prevail before the creation, or a worse one afterwards? And surely God must change, in that there must be a difference between God before creating the universe and God after creating the universe. Indeed, in that God knows the succession of changing events in the created universe, so God's knowledge changes. Augustine's solution in *Confessions* 11 is to reject the language of 'before' and 'after'. Time, he says, depends on change, because it is a measure of the relationship between objects and events that exist in succession in the created universe. God created time but does not exist in time: everything is present to God without variation or sequence. This solution generates new problems; for, if everything is eternally present to God, all possibilities must be fixed. Thus it is already certain that someone will, or will not, escape from sin. All these difficulties were linked with the basic Christian belief that God takes initiatives for the benefit of human beings, showing mercy for their sins and finally reconciling God and humanity in the person of Christ. In *Confessions*, Augustine seems much more concerned about creation than about incarnation.

Eventually (*C*. 8.1.1) Augustine went to seek advice from

Simplicianus, a friend of Ambrose. He explained that he had been reading Platonist texts and Simplicianus told him (*C.* 8.2.3) the story of Marius Victorinus who had translated them. This man was the perfect-role model for Augustine. He was another African, a teacher of rhetoric and a philosopher so distinguished that his statue stood in the Forum at Rome. He taught at Rome in the time of Constantine and came to accept Christianity after years of defending the traditional religion; but for some time he kept his beliefs private. When Simplicianus said that he would not believe Victorinus was a Christian until he saw him in church, Victorinus replied, 'Do walls make Christians?'. In the end he decided to go to church. The Roman clergy offered to let him make his profession of faith in private, to avoid embarrassment, but he made it before the congregation, all of whom knew him and rejoiced (*C.* 8.2.5). Augustine wanted to follow his example yet felt, he says (*C.* 8.5.12) like someone who wants to get up but is overcome by the pleasure of sleep and murmurs, 'Yes, in a minute'.

Augustine's intellectual position had changed. But the decision he saw as critical was that of living in chastity and renouncing the marriage which would have financed his ambitions. Eventually the decision was prompted (*C.* 8.6.13) by another of the apparently chance happenings which, in retrospect, he saw as having shaped his life. Another fellow-African, a court officer called Ponticianus, dropped in on him and Alypius because he wanted a favour. He picked up a book that lay on a gaming table: it was the letters of St Paul.

Ponticianus, a Christian who had a profession and a family, told the story of how two of his colleagues in the imperial civil service, taking a break from work at the western capital Trier, had come upon a small household of 'servants of God'. This was something new for the western empire in the mid-fourth century. In Egypt, perhaps a century earlier, Antony had set the example of abandoning property, and the distracting social and family duties that went with it, to live in the desert as a solitary (*monachos*, hence 'monk') devoted to prayer. Other monks chose to live in single-sex, austere communities. Stories of these Desert Fathers inspired westerners to follow suit. The monks at Trier had a copy of the life of Antony, perhaps in the Latin translation by Jerome's friend Evagrius. It inspired the civil servants to renounce their profession and join the monks: why, they asked, should they manoeuvre to stay in the emperor's favour, when they could become friends of God for the asking? Their fiancées followed their example and chose virginity; their married friends turned sadly back to their careers.

This story made Augustine painfully conscious of all the years in which he had postponed his search for wisdom in favour of worldly success and sexual pleasure, praying, in effect, 'Give me chastity and continence, but not yet' (*C.* 8.7.16). He was still unable to make the break with his past life until he was liberated by divine intervention. He heard a voice 'like a child's' calling, 'Take and read'; what he read in Paul's letters was a verse exhorting chastity. He was now able to abandon his wish for marriage and for worldly success (*C.* 8.12.30). For him this was liberation, just as Alypius was liberated from addiction to watching bloodshed. The rest of his narrative moves very swiftly, as if it too has been freed from the struggle with confusion and compulsion. Augustine resigned his post unostentatiously (*C.* 9.2.2-4) at the end of term, pleading ill health, and went to stay at Cassiciacum in a country house belonging to his friend Verecundus, with a group of family and friends. There he read the Psalms and argued with Alypius, who thought, apparently for reasons of style rather than theology, that he should not mention Christ in the books he was writing (*C.* 9.4.7-8). The philosophical dialogues that he wrote in this time at Cassiciacum do mention Christ, intense prayer and the singing of hymns and psalms; but they are Ciceronian in style and deploy allusions to Virgil, whom Augustine was reading with two pupils, rather than to the Bible. Looking back, Augustine saw these books still 'breathing hard' (*C.* 9.4.7) like someone who has not yet got his breath back after strenuous exercise. In *Confessions* Augustine's account of his time at Cassiciacum is concerned with his emotional response to the Psalms. In his treatise *On Order*, written at Cassiciacum, he explains his plan for a sequence of treatises on the liberal arts, to show how they prepare the way to philosophical wisdom. It seems that Augustine saw his conversion quite differently in 386, when he resigned his post, and in 395, when he wrote *Confessions* in the knowledge of what had happened since. As he tells the story, he and his friends decided only after their baptism to live as 'servants of God' in Africa (*C*. 9.8.17). He does not mention other options: a life of study and simplicity, like that which Cicero recommended for those who had resigned public office, and like that which they had themselves led at Cassiciacum; or a place in the monastic community founded by Ambrose (*C*. 8.6.15).

Augustine returned to Milan about five months later, when the time came to give in his name for baptism (*C*. 9.6.14). The rest of book nine is remarkable for its handling of memory and time, the problems that preoccupy Augustine in books ten and eleven. Augustine does not discuss how Ambrose prepared him for baptism: he returns and is baptised with Alypius and with his son Adeodatus, who was then about fifteen. Baptism was a new birth for them all: 'We joined Adeodatus with us as our contemporary in Your grace, to be brought up in Your education'. Adeodatus, who died young, dominates the brief account of the baptism. Augustine praises his exceptional intelligence and comments that his life as a boy and a young man gave no cause for anxiety. He does not explicitly say 'unlike my own'; instead, he says that baptism freed him from unease about his past life. He was deeply moved by thinking about God's salvation of humanity and by sharing in the music of the church at Milan. This brief allusion to profound religious emotion leads, unexpectedly, to a digression into history.

Augustine explains why Ambrose had introduced the eastern custom of congregational hymn singing, adopted by many or most churches at the time when Augustine was writing (*C*. 9.7.15). It was to encourage his congregation, which included Augustine's mother Monica, when they occupied a church to prevent its being taken over for worship by Arian Christians. Justina, mother of the boy emperor Valentinian, wanted the church for that form of worship, and Augustine goes on to describe how her anger was checked only when Ambrose located the bodies of two martyrs, Gervasius and Protasius, and miracles accompanied the movement of their remains to his basilica (*C*. 9.7.16). Then he asks the question that has probably occurred to his readers: why is he telling this story now? 'Whence and where have you led my memory, so that I confess to you these events too, when I had forgotten them, great as they are, and passed them over? At that time, when the fragrance of your perfumes was so strong, I was not running after you.' In more prosaic language, he was not part of Ambrose's congregation during these events and the discovery of the relics was not important to him when it happened in June 386; he was baptised at Easter 387. Is he trying, nevertheless, to associate himself with these great events in the church at Milan? Or is he deliberately collapsing times, in his own life, his son's life, and the life of the church, so that they all come together at the time of his rebirth in baptism? The next chapter (*C*. 9.8.17) suggests that the second interpretation is right. It brings in another friend from Thagaste, Evodius, who had already been baptised and had resigned his civil service post, and it provides a double conclusion to the travels of Augustine in a foreign country. 'We asked which place could most usefully have us as your servants: together we were going back to Africa. And while we were at Ostia on the Tiber, my mother died. I pass over many things, because I am in a great hurry.'

Monica's death prompts a brief biography, a sketch of her life with the emphasis on spiritual progress (*C*.9.8.17-9.22). Augustine describes a conversation they had had at Ostia and a shared spiritual ascent above the material world and even above discursive thought. After their reluctant return to the everyday world, Monica declares that she has no further purpose in life. She has even more that she had wished for, seeing her son not only a Christian but an ascetic Christian, a 'servant of God' (*C*. 9.10.26). She falls ill, and tells her sons that it does not matter where they bury her (*C*. 9.11.27-8). Augustine does not explain this sudden appearance of his brother. He spends time (*C*. 9.12.29-13.37) on his grief and recovery and on final prayers for his parents. Even his father, displaced earlier (*C*. 3.4.7) now rejoins the family, when Augustine refers to his baptism late in life. Just as Augustine did not describe the months he spent in Rome before moving to Milan, so he does not describe, in *Confessions* or elsewhere, the year he spent in Rome on his way back to Africa, waiting until the sea crossing was safe after yet another civil war. In the event he returned to Africa after only five years away. Milan had been geographically and spiritually the furthest point of his journey.

Return to Africa: monks and bishops

Confessions does not explain what happened after Monica's death and the story has to be reconstructed from other writings. Back in Thagaste Augustine formed a small community of friends in his family's house: it was probably the first monastery in North Africa. Like many other would-be monks (including, in the fourth century, Basil and John Chrysostom, both also brilliant speakers), he was pressed into a different kind of public service.

Each city, town or even large village in the empire had its bishop, who was a community leader as well as a preacher. In the first century CE, 'bishop' (from Greek *episkopos*, 'supervisor') was one of several possible titles for the people in authority in a Christian congregation. As the Christian churches reacted to doctrinal difference and to occasional persecution, it became standard practice to have one bishop as the leader and spokesman for a congregation; bishops in a given area would meet to decide policy. The local bishop became a public figure, the more so after Constantine declared his support for Christianity. Bishops were expected to use their contacts and influence to help their people; and they had an increasing workload of disputes in need of arbitration. At the council of Nicaea in 325 the assembled bishops had declared that men of high social status should not be hastily ordained, even if they were natural leaders by worldly standards; what the church needed was men with long experience of prayer and the Christian life. Local churches often saw it otherwise, as when the people of Milan demanded Ambrose the governor for their bishop. Augustine visited a friend at the seaport of Hippo, which he thought was safe because it already had a bishop. But the bishop alerted the congregation, Augustine was forcibly ordained priest, and (according to his biographer) when he wept for the loss of his monastic life, they thought he was crying from rage that he could not be bishop at once.

Bishops could not renounce the world. Ambrose did not believe in keeping the church out of politics; indeed he affirmed its moral authority to judge even the emperor. He excluded Theodosius I from communion for giving an order that resulted in the massacre of innocent people. On this occasion it may have been a staged 'repentance opportunity' in a difficult situation, but by the fifth century it had become a set piece in the relationship of church and state. Ambrose was endlessly busy trying to settle disputes, and Augustine did not dare interrupt his brief leisure, which he used for refuelling himself with food and study, with a plea for theological discussion (*C.* 6.3.3). Augustine himself, as bishop of a small coastal town, was drawn back into the world of lawsuits and contacts. In one of a group of letters rediscovered in the 1980s, he can be seen trying to find out the exact state of the law on slavery and to get it enforced against illegal trading, though without the brutal flogging that would probably kill the slavers. He found himself pleading with judges and commanders to stay in their jobs, exercising what mercy they could and refraining from anger and hatred in the task of preserving the civil peace.

Augustine had three years in his monastic community before he was ordained. During this time his son died, aged eighteen. There is nothing to show whether his brother and sister were important in his life at Thagaste. After his ordination he lived at Hippo, still in a small community of men, in a clergy house with a garden beside the cathedral. Although preaching was the bishop's job, Augustine was asked to do it even when he was a priest, not only at Hippo but also when the local clergy met. Bishop Valerius of Hippo did not want to lose him and, as soon as he could, perhaps five years later, arranged for Augustine to be ordained assistant bishop with the right to succeed him. This was irregular, but Valerius probably did not know that the council of Nicaea had forbidden it; for, when Augustine was challenged, he found it difficult even to get an accurate copy of the canons (rulings) of Nicaea.

Augustine's consecration as bishop confronted him with his past. People remembered his Manichaean connections and were not convinced that he had broken from them. They had no proof of his baptism at Milan and Ambrose had not asked his home church for letters attesting his fitness for baptism. The rival Donatist church was ready to use any weapon against him. North

African Christians were divided for historical and theological reasons, which were often scarcely understood but gave a pretext for feuding. The dispute began when Constantine became emperor and the persecution of Christians ended. The Donatists (named for one of their later leaders, Donatus) argued that anyone who had given way under persecution, even to the extent of handing over copies of the Bible to the police, was a source of contamination to the 'gathered church' of the righteous. The new bishop of Carthage had, they said, been consecrated by one of these 'betrayers' and they chose a rival bishop of what they considered to be the true church. The schism continued and worsened. Opposed to the Donatists were the Catholics: their name means 'universal' (Greek *katholikos*) but the 'universal' church was the minority church in Hippo and in much of North Africa. Families and communities were divided between Catholics and Donatists; Augustine's mother had Donatist relatives. Both sides committed murder, maiming and lynching and each blamed the other for bringing the power of the state to bear on the concerns of the church. Government intervention repeatedly failed to end the violence.

Augustine, in his first years as bishop, had to demonstrate both that he had rejected Manichaeism and that Donatism was theologically wrong in excluding sinners from the church. He wrote extensively on both subjects at all levels, from public controversy to academic debate. Meanwhile, he had to keep up his preaching and pastoral work for an ordinary congregation in a modest provincial town, act as theological consultant to a province and respond to intelligent Christians or non-Christians in search of discussion. He knew that he had come late to Christianity and that he was still in constant need of God's help. In the midst of all this, he wrote *Confessions*.

Part 2

Describing a life

'The first ten books are about me ...'

What kind of book is *Confessions?* As the reader begins, the answer is not obvious. Augustine starts from his impulse to praise God: 'You rouse us so that it delights us to praise you, because you made us for yourself, and our heart is restless until it is at rest in you' (*C.* 1.1.1). Immediately, he has a problem to put to God. Which comes first – invoking God or praising God? Is it possible to invoke God unless you first know God? How do you know whom you are invoking? He finds an answer: calling upon God is itself an act of belief in God. But this raises more problems. To invoke (Latin *invocare)* is to call in: how can Augustine 'call in' God, who made heaven and earth? Into what, and from where? Augustine would not exist if God were not in him or, rather, if he were not himself in God; and how can there be any place where God is not? God has said in the book of the prophet Jeremiah, 'I fill heaven and earth'. So what exactly does this mean?

Here is someone, alert to philosophy and language, trying to understand what he is doing, which is praising God. The dominant questions of the first chapters are 'What are You?' and 'Who am I?'. Augustine says (*C.* 1.6.7), 'I do not know where I came from'. He then moves abruptly to what seems to be the beginning of human life, the infancy which he cannot remember but can reconstruct from his parents' stories and from watching other babies (including, no doubt, his own son). The rest of Book one reflects on his infancy and childhood as manifestations of human greed, disobedience and social corruption. It is extraordinarily vivid but also detached from any particular context. Only later (*C.* 2.3.5) is there, suddenly, a local habitation and a name: Augustine's father Patricius, a modest family from Thagaste, school at Madaura, plans for education at Carthage.

Is this autobiography? Books one to nine of *Confessions* follow the same overall pattern as the opening chapters. There is a chronological sequence from infancy to death – that is, the death of his mother Monica, which comes soon after his abandonment of his former life and his rebirth as a Christian. Every so often Augustine tells readers where he is now (Carthage, Rome, Milan, Ostia), how old he is, what students he is teaching, though these mentions are always very brief and sometimes out of sequence. Dislocations of time are especially noticeable in the climax of his story, the account of his baptism. He recalls books he read and conversations he had; but what he spends time on is the beliefs he held about God, the reasons why he held them, and the questions they raise. He tries out and discards ideas, as in a philosophical treatise. 'Is this the answer? But, if so ...', always referring the question to God and accompanying it with acknowledgement of his own faults, appeals for further understanding, and praise.

So *Confessions* is intellectual or spiritual autobiography: there is no real difference, because Augustine's spiritual and intellectual life cannot be separated. It is the record of what a very intelligent man thought about God at different times of his life, made more convincing because readers can imagine the person he was when he held these beliefs. It is not concerned with other aspects of his life. To make a biography that fits present-day expectations, the outline narrative found in *Confessions* has to be filled out and the settings described, often from other writings by Augustine himself. That does not answer all the questions raised by *Confessions*. Autobiographies often end with some decisive moment – commitment to a career, a marriage, a philosophy – at some distance from the author's present lifestyle, which may not seem to him or her quite so interesting. That would explain why the narrative (such as it is) of Augustine's life ends at book nine as he waits to return to Africa after his mother's death. But what can readers make of the remaining books? Augustine said that books one to ten are about him. What is the function of book ten, and why should he add three books of biblical exegesis?

All kinds of narrative patterns have been found in *Confessions* but it is less easy to find an overall plan. Many critics think that

Augustine initially wrote an autobiography (books one to nine) ending with the decisive year of his conversion and his mother's death. The end of book nine is a valediction to Monica and *Confessions* together; it can be read as a dedication of the work, saying in effect, 'In memory of my parents, who brought me into this life, and especially my mother who saw me a Christian before she died'. His readers wanted more, so he added book ten to answer, or fend off, questions about his present life, while books eleven to thirteen are an appendix. People who think this often admit that they do not know why these books are there. This seems very unsatisfactory. An appendix needs a reason, usually that it contains material too technical or too tangential to fit in the main text. But Augustine was quite passionately interested in the content of books eleven to thirteen; if they were too technical to fit with an autobiography, he could have used the material in other theological writings.

Perhaps, then, it is a mistake to think in terms of 'adding books of exegesis'. If *Confessions* is spiritual autobiography, then Augustine's present theological position is obviously relevant – or, more strongly, it is the whole point. He might be writing apologia, an explanation of how he came to hold his present beliefs and a defence against those who suspected him of holding others. Or he might be using a technique of evangelism that he recommended for converts undergoing instruction. His strategy was to show at least some of the wonderful things God had done in one human life, by means of dreams, visions, interventions of one kind or another; then, having established the point that God is active in human lives, he could expound his present understanding of Christian teaching. This was an impossible programme for one book, even with frequent decisions to leave things out or acknowledgements of how much has been forgotten. Augustine begins at the beginning and scarcely gets beyond the first few verses of the first book of the Bible. This still allows him to cover an astonishing range of theological material. Augustine had been a *grammaticus*, used to taking students through texts: 'If my voice and pen confessed to you everything you explicated for me on this question, which of my readers would endure to receive it?' (*C.* 12.6.6). If that is the overall purpose, the life story which most readers find so fascinating was not, from Augustine's point of view, the most important part of *Confessions*. It was chiefly a preparation for books eleven to thirteen, which many readers skip.

It is also unsatisfactory to treat book ten simply as an update. If book ten is really a response to enquiries about what Augustine is like now, it must have disappointed the curious. Even when he acknowledges (in very discreet language, *C.* 10.30.41) that dream memories of sexual activity still prompt seminal emissions, he moves at once to the problematic relationship between himself awake, when such images have no effect, and himself asleep. He is not concerned to tell readers how he actually spends his days as bishop of Hippo, settling lawsuits, answering letters, trying to think about his next sermon, and attending endless conferences about Donatists. The one thing they learn about his life as a bishop is that he worries about music in church (*C.* 10.33.49-50): it encourages the faithful; but does it distract their fallible bishop from the content of the service? What he does, as usual, is to talk about his spiritual condition and to reflect on his own activity. He does so this time on a larger scale, which is signalled by a kind of second preface, recalling and restating the themes of the earlier books. Book one begins with the problem of invoking God who is beyond human knowledge, book ten with a prayer to 'know as I am known'. Once again, Augustine moves between narrative and reflection on what he has been doing; and what he has been doing in books one to nine is remembering his past in confession to God, though he also has in view a human audience, whom he gradually acknowledges. So he reflects on the reasons for doing this (to arouse love for God in himself and others) and on the activity of remembering. What and how does he remember, forget, transpose, reinterpret? This generates more questions about our experience of time and about the oddity of presenting the eternal God within a temporally ordered account, which in turn generates questions about creation and time and an attempt to understand the account of creation in Genesis. He continues to confess but the content of his confession is now his faith, his partial understanding and the darkness that is not yet illuminated (*C.* 11.2.2).

In fact Augustine makes it quite clear (*C.* 11.2.2) what he is doing. It is impossible for him to report the promptings by which God made him a Christian. He wants to use such time as he has to 'meditate on God's law', to acknowledge what he does and does not understand, i.e. to do theology. This is what, given the chance, he now is – a man, still subject to the distractions he has noted in book ten, who wants to know God. 'I do not want the hours to flow away to anything else, those that I find free from the needs of restoring the body, of concentrating the mind, and of the service we owe to people or do not owe but still pay.'

So it is misleading to think of Augustine adding books of exegesis to a work which is essentially autobiography. This is spiritual autobiography, as much concerned with his present beliefs as with his past. Yet the question remains: what kind of book is it? What was his envisaged audience, what signals would they pick up, and what expectations would he raise?

We do not know why Augustine wrote *Confessions* or how he would have described what he was doing. It is very difficult, as successive editors and translators have found, to summarise the content of any one book of *Confessions* or even to provide an uncontroversial running title at the top of any one page. Either they leave out something important or they produce so detailed a paraphrase that it is hardly a summary. Similarly, the style of *Confessions* moves in and out of different 'registers' even within a sentence – impassioned prayer, quiet narrative, Bible texts quoted, recombined and expounded, philosophical analysis of some particular problem, evocation of the classical canon. This is polyphony, not a clear melodic line.

Moreover, there are cross-connections with a very wide range of theological work on which Augustine was, or had been, engaged. He preached regularly on the Psalms, the part of Scripture he had thought about most. He had read them with great emotion after he made his commitment to Christianity (*C.* 9.4.8-11) and they were recited in the daily worship of the communities in which he lived at Thagaste and Hippo. They supply much of the biblical intertext of *Confessions*, the allusions and quotations that call to mind the experience of Augustine and his readers; and they supply a distinctive language for talking to God. Augustine was also doing other work on Genesis, a text he could not leave alone. The final books of *Confessions* are influenced by the beginnings of his theologically demanding *On the Trinity* (*C.* 13.11.12 summarises its main theme). He was also writing *Genesis Word by Word* (*de Genesi ad litteram*, often translated 'Literal Interpretation of Genesis') and he was moving between the different levels of meaning and interpretation that he discusses in *Confessions* 11-13. He had been lecturing on St Paul's Letter to the Romans, a text which insists that we cannot escape from sin unless God liberates us by grace; and that we may not question God's choice of those who are to be saved. It had transformed Augustine's own thinking on the need for God's grace and the way he interpreted his past life. His position had been clarified by questions on free will put by his old friend Simplicianus, who was now bishop of Milan, and by the continuing debate with Donatists who claimed to be the one true and righteous church. He had also convinced himself, in the first books of *Christian Teaching*, that rhetoric can be used to expound Christian truth and in *Confessions* he uses all the rhetorical skill he can muster.

Why, then, add to all this work a book 'about me'? One answer is that reflection on his past life offered Augustine yet another mode of doing theology. In *Confessions* he can demonstrate the use of the Psalms, and of Scripture generally, to interpret human life. He can show how Scripture, like a human life, can be interpreted on many levels, how wrong or inadequate interpretations of Scripture can distort a human life, as his own had been distorted by the crude readings and rejections taught him by the Manichaeans. It is a principle of interpretation for him that not only words but also events can be a 'figure' for other events, just as many episodes in the Old Testament were taken to prefigure events of the New Testament. So one man's life, described with exceptional vividness, can – to change the metaphor – be a microcosm, a small-scale example of alienation from God and redemption by God's active love. Similarly the workings of one man's mind and memory can help us rise to an understanding of the nature of God, as the Platonists taught; and one book can move from a narrative of one man's relationship with God to reflection on God's action in time and to human understanding of God's work.

Another answer is that *Confessions* is over-determined: there were simply too many reasons for writing it. Augustine was in his first few years as a bishop. He was very much a public figure. So it was necessary for him to come to terms with the expectation that he, a sinner in need of help, could bring God's word to his people. He was also living with his African past. So *Confessions* was an act of therapy but one which also needed to explain to others his past, especially the time he had spent away from Africa. Hostile critics had spread rumours about his Manichaean connection and doubts about his conversion, which he wanted to refute. Friends and admirers wanted to know how the successful rhetorician had returned to God, his homeland and an ascetic lifestyle. Their admiration was itself a danger, distracting them from awareness that Augustine, like them, was a person trying to live as God wants. Augustine wanted to give people a proper understanding of God's work in creation and redemption, to warn them off destructive errors that he knew only too well. One simple answer to the question 'What kind of book is this?' is 'It is a book about Augustine and what matters to him'. So perhaps we should rephrase the question and ask instead: 'What did Augustine, and Augustine's envisaged readers, think important in a life?'.

'I want to know all about you'

Who, then, were the expected readers of *Confessions*? It is an intellectually demanding book which assumes both a shared cultural background of literature and philosophy and a commitment to – or at least a strong interest in – Christianity. Apart from the circle of friends who had shared his life at Thagaste, did Augustine envisage many such readers in the African church or on its fringes? Perhaps he could expect a wider circulation for *Confessions*, through the ascetic networks of the late fourth century.

In the summer of 395, a year or so before Augustine started work on *Confessions*, his close friend Alypius (who also became a bishop, of Thagaste) wrote to Paulinus of Nola. Paulinus was a spectacular example of renouncing the world. He was a Spanish landowner, related to half the Roman aristocracy (including Ambrose), who had sold most of his estates, given the proceeds to the poor and retired to live chastely with his wife at Nola in southern Italy. Here he received pilgrims to the shrine of the little-known local saint, Felix; and from here he corresponded with other ascetic Christians, in a wonderful amalgam of late antique politeness and Christian self-deprecation, about the culture they shared as Romans and the Bible they shared as Christians. In case this sounds very depressing, he also had a sense of humour – witness his elaborate thanks for the gift of a camel hair cloak, as worn by John the Baptist. How many improving thoughts, he exclaims, will be inspired by its profitable bristles and salutary itch! His return gift – hopelessly inferior, of course – is a lambs-wool tunic.

Paulinus was an example to inspire Augustine and Alypius. It was Alypius who decided to make contact. He sent Paulinus some anti-Manichaean works of Augustine, perhaps in the hope of countering any damaging rumours, and asked for the *Chronicle* of the church historian Eusebius. Paulinus sent a copy, with a personal request.

> I particularly ask this of you: since you have embraced me, undeserving as I am, in your great love, that in return for this history of events you send me the whole history of your Sanctity, so as to declare 'of what race, from what homeland you come' called by so great a master, and from what causes 'separated from your mother's womb' you passed over to the mother of the sons of God who rejoices in her offspring, and joined 'a royal and a priestly people'. As you have mentioned that you learned the name of my lowliness at Milan, I admit to a special eagerness to learn – so that I may know you in all respects and be able to congratulate you the more – whether Ambrose, my father in that he took me up, invited you to faith or consecrated you priest, so that we both owe our being to the same man.
>
> [Paulinus, *Letter 3.4*]

Paulinus, like Augustine in *Confessions*, moves freely in and out of the two texts that were most important for the cultivated western Christian in the late fourth century. The first of his quotations is from the *Aeneid*, the second and third from the New Testament. 'Your Sanctity' and 'my lowliness' are Christian variations on a useful late antique convention in which the titles used express the approach of the person writing and what he hopes is true of the person addressed. An emperor, for instance, might have written to a civil servant, 'Our Benevolence sincerely hopes that Your Efficiency will soon be able to locate that file on tax concessions for teachers of rhetoric'. Both the style and the conscious modesty of Paulinus' letter create expectations for the tone of Alypius' reply.

Alypius was eager to establish a link with Paulinus, but he was too modest altogether to write about himself. So Augustine took over, just as (it appears from *Confessions*) he had taken the lead in so much of Alypius' life.

> Soon, with God's help, I shall put all of Alypius in your heart. What really worries me is that he would be afraid to reveal everything the Lord has done for him, in case a less intelligent reader – for such things would not be read by you alone – should take it not as God's gifts to humankind, but Alypius boasting about himself.
>
> [*Letter 27.5*]

Augustine likewise offers all of himself to Paulinus, as Paulinus in his letter has offered himself to them. Did Paulinus welcome this offer and is *Confessions* a response? It seems, at the very least, likely that this exchange of letters is one of the triggers for *Confessions* and that the account of Alypius in *Confessions* 6 is very much what Augustine wrote for Paulinus.

'I want to know all about you', in this context, has a quite specific content. Where are you from? How did you come to be a Christian priest or ascetic? Are you, too, one of Ambrose's followers? These are the familiar moves of people in the same profession establishing links. The questions do not ask for a narrative of personal history up to this point but for the aspects of one person's life which confirm and encourage others who are trying to do the same in theirs. Paulinus dismisses the time before he was a Christian in the letter quoted above: Ambrose

was the father who lifted the reborn Paulinus in his arms. In this
context the emphasis is not on personal achievement but on what
God has done for this person. Moreover it can be assumed that
the account is not marked 'private and confidential' but will be
passed on to other readers with similar interests and connections.
Fourth-century ascetics were much given to networking. It was
not only the most efficient method of getting books, as in Alypius'
request to Paulinus; but it was also a way of keeping in touch with
spiritual developments.

The account of Alypius in *Confessions 6* is shaped by these
expectations. Readers are told briefly that Alypius was from
the same town as Augustine, from a leading municipal family,
and that he was Augustine's student at Thagaste and Carthage,
studying rhetoric as a necessary part of law. What follows is
concerned with Alypius' progress, very much under the influence
of Augustine, to Christian commitment. His addiction to gladiator
fights, which can be overcome only by God, is balanced by a story
of his wrongful arrest at Carthage, which taught him not to be
hasty in condemning the apparently guilty, and by praise of his
integrity as a lawyer. He resisted bribery and intimidation; also
the temptation, which Augustine must have understood all too
well, to get books which he wanted for himself copied, free of
charge, by the government scribal staff he was entitled to use for
official documents. Alypius' theological progress is linked with
Augustine's but described in far less detail. Augustine does not
linger on the damage he must have done to Alypius and other
admirers who followed him into Manichaeism. Alypius was
baptised with Augustine (*C.* 9.6.14), and there the story ends.

Confessions includes another small-scale biography, the
account of Monica (*C.* 9.8.17-13.37) that follows the report of
her death. Perhaps, again, Augustine was reusing material he
had written for another purpose, something to replace the funeral
laudation he might have given had she died in Africa. Monica
is constantly praised for her profound Christian confidence and
her unremitting devotion to the son whose defection hurts her so
badly. Post-Freudian readers may find this a damaging mix of
possessiveness and criticism, but readers in the late fourth century
would be more likely to agree with Ambrose (*C.* 6.2.2) in telling

him how lucky he was. Yet Augustine's obituary for his beloved mother is not the life of a saint; for even Monica is shown to have weaknesses. As a child, strictly brought up, she almost becomes addicted to wine. Wine was the only mood-altering substance that was generally available in the ancient world and it was seen as one of the greatest dangers for women, since it weakened their chastity. Monica escapes the danger because one of the slaves shames her out of it. In Italy she has to shed some mistaken traditions of African Christianity; she does this willingly when instructed by Ambrose, though Augustine observes that she might have been less responsive to a different bishop (*C.* 6.1.1-2.2).

Above all, Monica has to abandon the worldly hopes for her son which had dictated too many of her responses to his conduct. She should have seen him safely married (*C.* 2.2.3, 2.2.8) once sexual desire began to trouble him: no doubt she was looking higher than a respectable girl from the provinces. Augustine uses Virgil to suggest that her feelings when he left Carthage for Italy were not wholly admirable. In the hope of avoiding a scene, he set sail when she was not expecting it, having falsely told her that he was seeing off a friend. He left her lamenting (*C.* 5.8.15) on the shore at Carthage. When Aeneas similarly slipped away from Carthage, leaving Dido frantic with grief and frustrated love, he was obeying the gods and carrying out his mission to found Rome. Dido was, however understandably, in the wrong, a woman in whom passion had displaced awareness of her own duty to her people and of the overall plan of the gods. Monica's grief is presented as loss, combined with anxiety that her son was taking the wrong path, but its intensity suggests that she was allowing feeling to displace faith. She follows Augustine to Italy and arranges a marriage (*C.* 6.13.23) which will further his career. He has to send away the woman he has lived with since his student days and replaces her (*C.* 6.15.25) with a temporary sexual partner. Once again, though he does not say so, his mother's worldly good sense has made him fall into sin. It is Augustine's conversion, his decision to live in chastity and abandon his career, that also liberates Monica from her worldly ambitions for him.

The closure of Monica's story is imposed by her death but those of Augustine and Alypius are closed at that same point, as they wait for passage home to Africa to lead a life in God's service. *Confessions* tells us nothing of the months they spent in Rome, of their life as members in a pioneering monastic community back at Thagaste or of their work as priest and bishop. Instead, Augustine talks entirely in terms of spiritual problems and God's help. Images of past sexual activity (*C.* 10.30.41), hunger which needs to be satisfied without excess (*C.* 10.31.43-7), praise from admirers (*C.* 10.37.60-2), are all hazards which he needs help to negotiate. There is nothing about the daily life of the overworked bishop of a minority church in a territory where religious disputes often became personal and local feuds. Augustine's past did not include a commitment to Donatism, so *Confessions* does not discuss the hazards of Donatist theology. Nevertheless, the kind of life story that would interest Paulinus also had its uses in Augustine's immediate situation. The Donatists claimed to be the one true church in Africa and in the world, the 'gathered church' of the righteous. That claim is tacitly challenged by Augustine's insistence that human beings are not righteous but are slaves of sin, freed only by the action of God. This is true of Alypius, of Monica, and above all of Augustine himself. They all have failings. They all need God's help throughout their lives.

Spiritual biography

The autobiography of *Confessions,* then, has a particular focus. Past life, even present lifestyle, is important only in so far as it displays God's mercy and explains the spiritual state of the person who is now struggling to live a God-centred life. To find something comparable to *Confessions*, we should not look to the biographies of powerful men written in the early second century by Suetonius in Latin, by Plutarch in Greek, even if there were any evidence that Augustine read them. The closest precedents and parallels come from the philosophical tradition of examining one's own conduct, especially from the soul-searching of Christian ascetics.

After Constantine declared his support for Christianity, there were no more martyrs condemned by Roman government. Some Christians embarked on the 'long martyrdom' of ascetic life. A literature of renunciation and spiritual struggle recorded their progress. The *Life of Antony* was available in Latin translation from about 370. Ponticianus, who told the story of the two civil servants who came upon a copy of it at Trier (*C.* 8.6.15), was very surprised that Augustine and Alypius had never heard of it. Other 'Desert Fathers' besides Antony inspired collections of sayings and brief life-stories, and these too were in circulation in the late fourth century. Augustine's contemporary Jerome wrote a life of Paul the hermit, supposedly a predecessor of Antony. Jerome also wrote letters, obviously designed for public reading, about his own attempts at the ascetic life, up country from Antioch in the desert of Syria. Later generations of painters showed him kneeling in anguished penitence among rocks, alone but for a patient lion (who had migrated from the story of a saint with a similar name). Jerome tells how his love for classical literature distracted him from the Bible, how he found his fellow-ascetics confrontational, how he missed his friends and how the empty expanse of the desert became filled with visions of dancing girls. Another letter (*Ep.* 108) is in effect a saint's life, of his friend Paula. This woman, a member of the Roman aristocracy, abandoned her worldly life and her three children, sailing away to visit the monks of Egypt and founding two monasteries in Bethlehem, for herself and Jerome. In Jerusalem, another Roman aristocrat who had abandoned her family, Melania the elder, founded monasteries for herself and for the ascetic Rufinus. Her granddaughter, Melania the younger, also renounced her worldly wealth – a process which meant selling off properties in Rome and many other areas of empire, including Thagaste, where, according to her biographer, her estate was rather bigger than the town.

   This literature of admiration carried spiritual risks for its subjects; it often records that they recognised the danger of pride. 'Hagiography' originally meant 'writing about saints'; now, for good reason, it means 'uncritical admiration'. The information Augustine gives in *Confessions* could, if handled by an admiring outsider, turn into hagiography; and in a biography by the devoted Possidius, a member of the community at Hippo, Augustine does become a paragon. This hazard may explain why Alypius lost his nerve about telling Paulinus his story, and why Augustine refused to end *Confessions* at book nine, as if, once converted, he had achieved instant sanctity and lived happily ever after. By addressing God in praise and admission of weakness, Augustine avoids the dangers of pride and self-reliance, of attention to his own achievements, and of belief that the achievements were his own.

Christians who seemed to others to be spiritual heroes were themselves overwhelmingly aware of weakness and danger. Christian ascetics of the later fourth century developed a remarkable collective experience of self-examination, some of which was recorded in classic guides to the spiritual life. The most famous of these, by Evagrius Ponticus (who classified the seven deadly sins) and John Cassian, had great influence on later monastic tradition. Ascetics, who lived in solitude or in communities organised for prayer, work and Bible study and who sought advice from those spiritually more advanced, became intensely conscious of the desires and failings that separated them from God. They felt themselves to be under attack by the forces of evil that could exploit the weaknesses of a human heart not yet committed wholly to God. They did not dare to suppose that they would not succumb. They told the story of the monk who, after years of lonely struggle against lust, was found racing off to town in search of a prostitute.

Antony advised monks to write down their actions and the promptings of their heart, as if for others to read, because the fear of being found out would help them even when their confession remained secret. Augustine's motivation is different. He knows he has readers and he hopes to encourage them if they think it is all too difficult and themselves too weak: of course they are, but help is at hand, as it is for him (*C.* 10.3.4). The predominant tone, the emphasis on weakness and uncertainty and the ever-present risk of sin, belongs not just to Christian late antiquity but to one particular strand within it and perhaps specifically to Augustine. Many people in his lifetime, notably the British ascetic Pelagius, thought he overdid the uncertainty; for baptized Christians could be sure that God would not let them go, nor would God have been so cruel as to give human beings commandments they could not follow. Pelagius was deeply shocked when he was told of Augustine's repeated prayer: 'You command continence: grant

what you command, and command what you will' (*C*. 10.29.40).
It seemed to him that Augustine's acknowledgement of God's
grace had gone too far towards professed helplessness, as if God
had not given us the Bible for instruction and each of us the ability
to reflect, establish good habits and make moral efforts. Pelagius,
in return, was accused of relying too much on human reason, in
the tradition of Greek and Roman philosophy.

Philosophers from Socrates on had encouraged their students
to think about what they were doing, what motives and desires
they were hiding from themselves, whether their life was rightly
directed. Aristotle, for instance, remarked that those who seek
high status are really trying to convince themselves that they
are worth something. A philosopher might decide that his life
needed radical change: 'conversion' from worldly concerns is not
peculiar to Christianity or to late antiquity. Stoic philosophers, in
particular, were taught to deal with the crises of life by assessing
their responses and deciding whether these were in accord with
their principles.

The most famous work in this tradition makes a revealing
contrast with *Confessions*. Its author was the emperor Marcus
Aurelius, in the mid-second century, and it is often known as the
Meditations of Marcus Aurelius. Its actual title is *To Himself* and
it is written as a personal notebook of self-exhortation and moral
comment. Some of it was written in a tent at the end of hard days
of campaigning on the northern frontier, when Marcus lacked the
philosophical books and companionship that would keep him on
the right lines. Marcus, like Augustine, noted events and people
who had made him what he was. He was grateful for the guidance
of the gods which, as he could see when he looked back, had
saved him from error. But his book belongs to a different moral
universe from Augustine's. Here is part of his first section, a short
retrospect of his life and what he owes to different people and to
the gods.

> From the gods: good grandparents, good parents, a good
> sister, good teachers, good family and friends almost
> without exception. I thank the gods that I did not offend
> against any of them, even though my temperament might

have made me do so: by the beneficence of the gods, no set of circumstances put me to the test. And that I was not brought up for any longer time by my grandfather's concubine, and that I did not become a man before due time, but if anything, rather late..../ That I had a brother whose character roused me to take care of myself and cheered me with respect and affection. That my children were neither defective in mind nor deformed in body. That I made no further progress in rhetoric, poetry and the other arts by which I might have been absorbed, had I found the path easy..../ That I did not touch Benedicta or Theodotus, and in later life recovered from passion. That although I was often angry with Rusticus, I did nothing that I might regret.   [*To Himself* 1:17]

This passage shows Marcus to be aware of his own temperament and his intellectual limitations, of the benefits he has received from the gods and the hazards they have helped him to avoid. He does not agonise, as Augustine does, about the experience of sexual desire and imperfect relationships, or the hazards of literary skill, as manifestations of human sin and alienation from God. He is grateful to the gods for what they have given him, without considering himself unworthy and corrupt. He tries to assess himself correctly and to be thankful that there are some problems he does not have.

The common assumption of this philosophical tradition is that we can analyse our motives and conduct; that, when shown our absurdity, we can behave better by deciding to do so and by establishing better habits. Socrates, according to Plato, said that no one willingly does wrong, and Aristotle offered an account of why people do things that they know to be wrong. He concluded that either they do not really know it to be wrong and are simply parroting what they have been told, or that they do know it but have temporarily lost sight of their knowledge under the influence of desire, drink or madness. It does not make sense to suppose that, if I really and at this moment know that murder is wrong and therefore destructive to me as well as my victim, I shall go ahead and do it. Many people in the fourth century CE shared such beliefs, including the more confident kind of Christian. But Christian ascetic tradition had far less confidence in the power of reason and good habits. The common experience of Greek and Roman philosophers was that the practice of philosophy brought them closer to God, but the common experience of committed Christians was – and is – that those who seem to outsiders to be closest to God are most acutely conscious of what separates people from God. Hence the anguish over aspects of human life which others take for granted; hence, too, the willingness to describe oneself as a sinful failure.

Many philosophers have thought that true human nature, uncorrupted by social pressures, appears in the human infant. The current western version of this 'cradle argument' is that the uncorrupted child eagerly explores his or her environment and responds to love. Augustine sees in human infancy both God's goodness, which ensures that the mother's response is matched to the needs of her child, and the beginnings of human alienation from God in greed and jealousy. Readers often feel that he overdoes the guilt: what, after all, is so bad about a baby who does not want another to be fed first (C. 1.7.11), or a gang of teenagers (C. 2.4.9, 2.6.12) stealing flavourless pears? As mothers and nurses told Augustine, 'Oh, he'll grow out of it.' And yet why was he like that in the first place? What has happened to human beings that a baby should grudge milk to his brother, who like himself would die without it, when there is plenty for both? Why should it be pleasurable to steal something you neither need nor even enjoy, just for the hell of it? Augustine would have made his readers think hard about that casual English phrase. Hell is alienation from God. 'Is *that* the innocence of childhood?' (C. 1.19.30).

Confessions, then, is most closely related to the philosophical tradition of self-examination, especially to the self-examination of Christian ascetics in the late fourth century. It is concerned with moral and spiritual development rather than with the events of a life. If it is called the first autobiography, that is because present-day readers expect an autobiography to be a life history revealing the inner feelings and self-awareness of the writer. Augustine's development of the tradition of self-analysis was made possible by a different understanding of human beings in relation to God and by a different religious language for talking to God. The Psalms, used in daily worship in Augustine's community, are songs that cry out in anguish, self-reproach, reproach of God, confidence and expectation of help from God. There is nothing like them in Greek or Latin literature.

Confessions depends on the assumption that what matters in a life – and, therefore, in the description of a life – is the attainment of goodness. Augustine shares this assumption with Greek and Roman philosophy; what he does not share is the expectation that an exact moral analysis is the basis for good habits of thought and is therefore most of the battle. He often describes an experience or a state of mind, then freezes his narrative while he discusses what exactly is happening. Even in the highly charged account of his conversion to a life of chastity, he stops (*C.* 8.9.21-10.24) to engage in careful and lucid discussion of a philosophical problem: what exactly is happening when I make an act of will but do not carry it out? Who or what is giving the instruction and resisting it? Are there actually two or more wills at work when there are conflicting choices to be made? It is very important here to reach the right conclusion: there is no alien force at work which is 'not the real me' and which can be discarded. There is one person trying to reach a decision. In the philosophical tradition – and in some people's experience – it is enough to state the problem correctly. Augustine, having demonstrated that he can do this with great efficiency, insists that his own experience shows it is, in itself, not enough. God has to intervene; for only then does it become possible to act and to understand what the direction of life has really been. If clarity is not enough, how can Augustine select and convey to his readers the true direction and the mis-directions of his life?

True *Confessions*? Narrative and memory

> How do they know, when they hear from me about me, whether
> I am telling the truth, since no one knows what is going on in a
> human being except the spirit of the human being, which is in
> him?   [*C*. 10.3.3]

But how does even the human spirit know what is going on, unless
God tells it the truth (*C*. 10.5.7)? Is there a definitive account of a
human life and can it be given during that lifetime by the person
who is living the life – or by anyone else? Augustine reiterates, at
critical moments in his story, that he could not see where he was
going, or why, or what was really important – like Robert Graves'
butterfly who 'lurches here and there by guess and God and hope
and hopelessness'. He also acknowledges that there are many
things he has forgotten or that he misunderstood at the time. In
book ten he breaks any dramatic illusion by making readers look at
the man who has told the story and who is still wrestling with temptation and confusion. He describes (*C*. 10.8.12) the experience of
searching his memory and finding that what comes to mind is not
what he wanted. So how can we believe his present confession?

Some of Augustine's first readers were prepared to accuse
him of deliberate lies or at least of misrepresentation. The senior
bishop of his region had expressed some (understandable)
anxieties about his ordination as bishop after so little experience
of the church, especially when nothing was known about his
baptism at Milan and rather too much was remembered about his
youth. His Donatist enemies, as well as his former Manichaean
friends, seized on this. A Manichaean, Secundinus, accused him
of leaving the sect only from fear of persecution, not because
their teachings had been refuted. A Donatist, Petilianus, said that
Augustine was still a crypto-Manichean and was further up the
hierarchy than a simple 'hearer'. He had left Carthage because
the governor expelled him (but Augustine could show that this
was wrong on dates). Moreover, he was still at heart a rhetorician
and an adept in dialectic, given over to pagan culture. In 403
Augustine had to defend himself at a church council in Carthage.

When he says (*C.* 10.3.3) that his fellow-Christians will, in charity, believe him, these accusations are the background. One message of book ten is: 'This is what I am now, not a Manichaean but a Christian seeking truth'.

Present-day critics ask different questions about Augustine's theology. Is he trying to maximise his connection with Ambrose and minimise his connection with the Milan Platonists? Why does he say so little about the content of Christianity? Was his conversion really to Platonism? They have also put forward a more radical challenge. Augustine may be trying to tell the truth, but suppose he has got it all wrong? From his perspective in the late fourth century, the guiding theme is God's intervention, often undetected at the time, to rescue a human soul from falsehood, error and the habit of sin. But some present-day readers think there is a different underlying story: Augustine is really describing, with unprecedented clarity, the problems that many people now find most interesting in human life, namely his relationship with his parents and his attitude to sexuality.

Augustine's father Patricius is not much in evidence in *Confessions* – nor, indeed, is any member of Augustine's family except his mother. Patricius is presented as a passionate man who disregards Christian teaching until very late in his life (*C.* 9.9.19, 22), and who rejoices when he notices, at the baths, that his son is capable of begetting sons (*C.* 2.3.6). Augustine's mother, on the contrary, tries to deny her son's sexuality, and, as Augustine himself puts it, to replace his earthly father by a father in heaven (*C.* 1.11.17). Patricius dies just as Augustine embarks on adolescent rule-breaking and sexual turmoil: his death is reported later in parenthesis (*C.* 3.4.7) and seemingly without emotion. Augustine is describing how he reached Cicero's *Hortensius* in the standard curriculum at Carthage and found it had transformed his ambitions.

> Suddenly, all empty hope was cheapened and I desired the immortality of wisdom with an incredible ardour in my heart and I began to rise up to return to you. So it was not to the sharpening of my tongue, which is what I seemed to be buying at my mother's expense – I was nineteen and

my father had died two years earlier – it was not, then, to
the sharpening of my tongue that I applied the book, nor
did it impress upon me its style but what it was saying.

'Rise up to return to you' evokes, for readers of the Bible, the
parable of the Prodigal Son. Augustine too decided to 'rise up
and return to my father', to go back to God. His earthly father is
dismissed both as a spiritual and as a practical force in his life.

By contrast, Thagaste is made intolerable by the death of a
friend (*C.* 4.7.12) who shared Augustine's passion for literature
and philosophy. This is characteristic of the relationships
described in *Confessions*; for in *Confessions* Augustine is never
alone, not even at times of intense emotion (*C.* 8.12.28, 9.12.31)
or when caught up in a vision (*C.* 9.10.24). Yet, even when we
know from other texts that family members were with him, the
people he talks about are those with whom he shared the pursuit
of knowledge. That, evidently, did not apply to his father, who
had found the money for his early education, whereas his son
Adeodatus (*C.* 9.6.14) was also his fellow student, a partner
even at the age of sixteen, in Augustine's dialogue *The Teacher*.
Augustine, touchingly, insists that the ideas Adeodatus advances
in the dialogue were his own, that he was unusually intelligent
and that there was nothing to cause anxiety in his boyhood and
adolescence. His early death is reported out of sequence and
Augustine says nothing of his own feelings, though the effect is
very different here from that of the dismissal of Patricius. The
death of Adeodatus is set in the context of his baptism, when he
and Augustine became contemporaries as newborn Christians
cleansed of sin (*C.* 9.6.14).

In *Confessions* Augustine takes the lead among his friends,
never finding an adequate tutor or a father figure in Carthage,
Rome or even Milan. Faustus the Manichaean is charming,
a pleasant companion in reading, but not educated or clever
enough (*C.* 5.13.23). Ambrose, Augustine's 'spiritual father' in
the sense that he baptised Augustine, is obviously too busy to
attend to his needs. When Augustine was becoming interested
in Christian doctrine, Ambrose read silently and did not talk to
him (*C.* 6.3.3). When Augustine sent in his name for baptism and

asked what he should read, Ambrose recommended another text, the prophet Isaiah, that Augustine could not understand (*C.* 9. 5.13). Augustine says nothing about advice from Ambrose after baptism when he and his friends were deciding what to do with their lives (*C.* 9.8.17). Virgil's Aeneas, who supplied Augustine with a model for his own journeys, left the ruins of Troy carrying his aged father on his shoulders and leading his little son by the hand. His father's advice and support sustained him through his first wanderings; he was devastated by his father's death and went down to the underworld to seek his advice; his son grew up to fight beside him. The father-son relationship seems more congenial and more important to Virgil than any other human relationship. But Augustine, who left his father behind at Thagaste, seems much better able to cope with the teacher-student relationship or with the quasi-parental and quasi-sibling connections of shared study than with being a father or a son.

This may be an unfair – or at least an overstated – interpretation. Augustine's father rejoins his wife and son at the end of book nine, united with them by baptism and in Augustine's prayer for his parents. Silence about family relationships can be explained. *Confessions* is concerned with Augustine's spiritual and intellectual progress to Christian commitment; so the people who most influenced his thinking must be the most prominent in his text. Teachers and students are bound to matter in the life of a professional teacher. Most young people are more concerned with their friends, who have chosen them, than with their parents. For Augustine the non-possessive love of friends is theologically as well as personally vital (*C.* 6.16.26). But present-day readers see danger signals in the intensely possessive love of his mother – the best-known mother in all classical literature, who is so constant a presence in *Confessions* books one to nine and whose death is the climax and the closure of the books. 'The son of all those tears can not be lost' (*C.* 3.12.21) can be read positively or negatively. The positive reading is that Monica's tears and prayers, her efforts to live by Christian principle and her physical presence in Thagaste, Carthage and Milan kept Augustine in contact with Christianity, however far – geographically or spiritually – he went away into foreign countries. (If Augustine had got further with Homer at school [*C.* 1.14.23], he might have evoked the weeping of Penelope which keeps Odysseus a presence in his home throughout his wanderings.)

The negative reading runs as follows. When Augustine goes home to teach after his time at Carthage, his mother, who now controls the family money, throws him out of the house because he is a Manichaean. Reassured by a vision (*C.* 3.11.19) in which he is standing beside her on a ruler – which she interprets to mean that he abides by the rule – she tries to keep him near her in Africa. 'The son of all these tears cannot be lost' was said by a sensible bishop who had himself grown out of Manichaeism and who was becoming tired of Monica's persistence (*C.* 3.12.21); perhaps he recognised the power of emotion rather than the power of prayer. Monica is with Augustine in Carthage when he leaves for Italy, not daring to tell her he is doing so and invoking in his narrative Aeneas abandoning Dido (*C.* 5.8.15). She recovers from despair and is with him again at Milan, where she succeeds in displacing his long-term partner with a fiancée who is too young to marry. Her triumph comes when he returns to the rule (*C.* 8.12.30), abandons both the career and the sexuality that took him from her and prepares for their return home together:

> Son, so far as I am concerned, nothing in this life delights me any more. I don't know what I still have to do here or why I am here: I have used up my hopes for this world. There was only one reason why I wanted to live on a little longer, to see you a Catholic Christian before I died. My God has given me that and more, so that I could see you as his servant, rejecting earthly happiness. What am I doing here?   [*C.* 9.10.26]

Monica and Augustine have been separated, like the lovers in ancient romances, by physical distance and by his enslavement (in this case to false teachings); his everlasting life has been in danger. Now they are united in a shared vision (*C.* 9.10.23). Monica can die in peace, and Augustine, who mentioned his father's death in parenthesis and his son's in a few brief sentences, describes with intense and lengthy recall his reaction to her death (*C.* 9.12.29-31).

He is left obsessed with sexuality as the manifestation of human sin and with the need for reconciliation through knowledge with a father-God. He cannot understand this father's purposes, and the only response to his pleas and questions is in the words of a text which he must correctly interpret or perish. (Perhaps that explains books twelve and thirteen.) In the same way, the worldly future of the child Augustine once depended on understanding Virgil, who supplied him with images of destructive love and of journeys in obedience to a stern father.

This second reading cannot be refuted but it will not satisfy any reader who thinks that God is more than a projection of psychic impulses. Late Roman culture offers plenty of ammunition for post-Freudian interpretation. Sons, even adult sons, were expected to obey their fathers. The father's authority to instruct and punish, as head of household, is one of Augustine's dominant images for the ordering of society. The child's entry into human society, he observes in *Confessions* 1, is marked by coercion: the baby cries, the schoolchild is beaten. Augustine swings between a characteristic conviction that it was all his fault and a return to the child's resentment of false adult values. 'The amusement of adults is called business', he remarks (*C.* 1.9.15). Grown-ups spend hours at the games and punish their children for neglecting schoolwork; they refuse to take seriously beatings which are a real terror to their children; and, whatever they say, they mind more about manners and worldly success (*C.* 3.3.5) than about morals. Augustine reflects in book ten on the oddity of remembering emotion without feeling it but in the books about his childhood (as often in autobiography) emotion is very strong.

Sons were also expected to defer to the wishes of mothers. The tradition of Roman motherhood was to show commitment to children by strong moral concern and by fair-mindedness in assigning property; also by urging sons to the achievements that society denied to women. Personal nurture in childhood, encouragement of the children's interests, leaving them space to grow in the confidence that their parents accept them for what they are – all this is a very recent ideal for the middle-class mother. So is the ideal of marriage as a strong emotional commitment chosen by the parties. In Roman society marriage was, by definition, a relationship for the procreation of legitimate children. It was usually negotiated by families. Affection and respect were likely to develop if both parties behaved well. As far as the children were concerned, in a society without welfare provision, the emphasis was on their deference to the reasonable wishes of the parents who invested money and effort in them, not on love and self-determination.

Present-day readers almost always condemn Augustine for sending away his concubine so that his mother could negotiate a marriage to someone who was still a child. Augustine and the concubine had a longstanding and sexually fulfilling relationship (*C*. 4.2.2, 6.15.25); they had a son; he was deeply wounded by losing her; but he never even tells us her name. How could he? And yet, by fourth-century standards, what else could he do? It was quite usual to arrange a betrothal before one or both of the parties was ready for marriage. The legal age of marriage for a girl was twelve and it was assumed that she was then biologically mature. It was also usual for a man to delay marriage until he was established in a career; and far more respectable for him to have a live-in partner than to resort to prostitutes or (much worse) pursue other men's wives or daughters.

'Live-in partner' imports modern assumptions, as do 'mistress', 'lover' or 'girlfriend'. The Roman technical term 'concubine' means a woman who is not married but is the acknowledged partner of one man, who is therefore the acknowledged father of her children. Men had, as a rule, good reason for not marrying their concubines. The most usual reason was that the relationship was never intended to produce children (cf. *C*. 4.2.2). Sometimes the woman could not make a legal marriage, because she was a slave or had started out as an actress or entertainer. If she could legally marry but had to settle for less, she was very likely to belong to the lower classes in a society that formalised class distinction in law. The 'lower orders' (*humiliores*) could be tortured to give evidence as slaves were; they suffered physical punishments which the 'more respectable' (*honestiores*) were spared. Marriage to the concubine would have meant the abandonment of all Augustine had worked for and Monica had financed. Nor could he have continued to live with a concubine once his marriage was arranged. It was taken for granted that men had casual sexual relationships with lower-class women or slaves; a permanent commitment would be an insult to the lawful wife. The family of Augustine's future bride would never have tolerated it.

Augustine's concubine was leading the best life she could by her fidelity to him and by her decision to live in chastity after they parted. It is a sign of respect, not of neglect, that he does not publicise her name. When he wrote *On the Good of Marriage*, he said that a man who dismisses a faithful concubine to marry another woman has committed what Jesus called 'adultery in the heart', and the adultery is against the concubine, not the intended wife. Not all Christians shared this opinion. Bishop Leo of Rome, in the mid-fifth century, authorised Christian men to dismiss a concubine and marry, on the grounds that this was not bigamy, but moral improvement. Augustine is not complacent about his own conduct: he knew it was not to his credit (*C.* 4.2.2, 6.12.22) that he was held by a sexual bond instead of a commitment to raise children.

Augustine's views on sexuality are rooted in late Roman culture. It was a philosophical commonplace, dating back to Plato, that sexual activity binds humans to the body and diverts energy from the exercise of reason. Augustine was not alone in pointing out that sexual response – or its absence – defies rational control. Many of his fellow-Christians thought that in his later theology he over-emphasised sexual guilt, as he did moral helplessness. Like their non-Christian contemporaries, they thought that sexual desire had its God-given use in the procreation of children within marriage. They were not prepared to think, as Augustine eventually did, that children are born infected with the lust which was biologically necessary for their conception – even though this 'original sin' is a tidy explanation for the greed and possessiveness that worried Augustine in little children. Augustine had to defend himself against the charge (derived in part from *Confessions*) that he was still Manichaean in his suspicion of sex. Nowadays he needs defending against the charge that his theology, indeed his Christian commitment, is the result of a childhood he was not equipped to understand.

Multiple readings and exegesis

Augustine could easily reply to this charge by asking (*C*. 10.3.3) how others can know what was actually happening in his life. He would have to admit that all he can offer is a reading of God's purposes. He confesses to God and appeals to God for enlightenment: *Confessions* is not a soliloquy addressed to himself but extended prayer addressed to God. God does not speak in this long conversation, except in the verses of Scripture that come to Augustine's mind, in the biblical intertext of his life. God has written a book and Augustine is happy with books, though a dominant theme of the *Confessions*, exemplified in the last three books, is that Scripture can be read in many ways and understood at different levels (*C*. 6.5.8). '"It means what I say." "No, it means what I say." I think there is more true piety in saying, "Why not both, if both are true, or a third or a fourth interpretation or whatever other truth anyone has ever found in these words?"' (*C*. 12.31.42).

The techniques of exegesis that Augustine learnt from Ambrose's preaching can be used on his own work. Augustine envisaged God not so much dictating the Bible as commissioning authors for its various books. He once, perhaps wistfully, speculates, 'If I had then been what Moses was, and You had assigned me the book of Genesis to write ...' (*C*. 12.26.36). For Augustine, a Biblical author's choice and ordering of words repay study, just as in school readings of Virgil or modern 'close readings'. Scripture has its own usages which are not necessarily those of ordinary speech. But the Bible is a corpus of texts which must be studied together (its Greek name, *ta biblia*, means 'the books', plural) and verses should be interpreted not in isolation but in context. The context is the full range of biblical teaching, even if the relevant author could not have known it. Thus Augustine, seeking to understand (*C*. 13.6.7-7.8) why the Spirit was 'borne above the waters' in Genesis 1.2, invokes phrases of St Paul on the 'supereminent' Holy Spirit (I Corinthians 12.1). He suggests that the Spirit lifts us above the waters: for Augustine water, especially sea-water, often symbolises the flux of living in the material world and the dissipation of attention away from God.

Apparent contradictions in Scripture can be resolved by attention to different levels of meaning. For instance, in *On the Trinity* Augustine rescues Paul from a charge of directly contradicting Genesis. Paul says (I Corinthians 11.7) that man is in the image of God but woman is the image and glory of man, whereas Genesis says God created humanity in God's own image: male and female God created them. Augustine concludes that Paul has in mind the physical inferiority of woman, which seemed to them both an obvious fact, whereas Genesis refers to the spiritual equality of male and female. Augustine summarised the principles of exegesis in *Christian Teaching*: if any verse of the Bible is not obviously teaching either good conduct or Christian faith, it should be interpreted allegorically.

Such techniques were not peculiarly Christian devices for 'saving the text' but were common to late antiquity. They were used also in Jewish interpretation of the Torah and in the attempts by Platonist philosophers to reconcile not just Plato and Aristotle but the traditions of mythology which Plato had condemned. Thus, in some Platonist writings, the horrific story of the god Kronos, who swallows his children, becomes an allegory of time (Greek *chronos*) absorbing what it produces so that the present is always becoming the past – a problem that interests Augustine in *Confessions* 11. But once it is accepted that there are connections, patterns and levels of meaning that may not have been apparent to the author, then the author cannot determine how the text is read. So Augustine, who in book thirteen interprets Moses as conveying truths about the Trinity and the Christian Church, is left without defence against a Freudian reading of his own text.

Unlike many of his present-day readers, Augustine believes that there is a control on multiple readings: there is truth authenticated by the word of God. He has a canon (Greek *kanon*, rule or standard of measurement) of both text and interpretation. Scripture is authoritative: readers cannot select, as the Manichaeans did, only the bits they like. It is acceptable to find in Scripture a meaning which the writer did not understand but which was foreseen by the Spirit who inspires the writer with truth. It is not acceptable to find a meaning quite other than the writer intended (*Christian Teaching* 3.27.38, 1.37.41). There are multiple interpretations of Scripture, but they must be measured against the rule of faith.

This is not a final reply, because of the problem known to theologians as the hermeneutic circle, the circle of interpretation. Scripture must be interpreted by the rule of faith but the rule of faith is itself formulated in accordance with Scripture. Augustine thinks he still has an answer: 'Moses wrote this, wrote it and went away' (C. 11.3.5). Suppose that Augustine, in his efforts to read Genesis, could question Moses himself, overcoming the initial problem that Moses speaks Hebrew:

> How would I know whether he was speaking the truth? If I did know, would it be from him? Within me, within the dwelling-place of my thought, truth neither Hebrew, Latin, Greek nor barbarian, without the instruments of mouth and tongue, without the sound of syllables, would say 'He speaks the truth', and I would at once, in full assurance, say confidently to that man of yours, 'You speak the truth.'

Readers have to decide whether they can say the same to Augustine.

Narrative and memory

Confessions, then, is a modern book in its awareness of the activity of reading and of multiple interpretations, not a post-modern book which would postulate that there are no correct readings. The Freudian reading of Augustine's experience is one possible interpretation of a book that can itself be read on many levels, as autobiography, philosophical theology, reflection on narrative, evidence of cultural transformation, evidence of a new sense of the self – and that is not an exhaustive list. All readings, however far they depart from Augustine's own interpretation of his life, depend on what Augustine chooses to tell. The problem of *Confessions* is that of any autobiography: by simplifying the complexities, ignoring the seemingly irrelevant, establishing a structure and a narrative sequence and a style, above all just by forgetting (C. 3.12.21), the author edits his or her life. It is literally impossible – not just unreadable – to 'tell it like it is', to record lived experience. Some writers make this point by selecting what is usually rejected: trivial events or chance associations of ideas. Augustine makes it by reflecting on the workings of memory.

Memory training is a very important part of education in rhetoric: successful speakers need a stock of examples and ready-made phrases; above all, they must remember the points they want to make. Feats of memory were much admired in late antiquity. Augustine's near contemporary Eunapius, who wrote short bio-graphies of sophists (professional intellectuals) and philosophers of the later fourth century, told the story of Prohaeresius defeating rival orators. He asked only for a serious topic, for shorthand writers and then for silence. He improvised a brilliant speech, then, as the shorthand writers confirmed, repeated it word for word.

One technique attested from the Renaissance (and still in use) was the *aedes memoriae* ('house of memory'). The student imagines a regular facade or building and puts the items he wants to remember in specified places: for instance, the successive points of a speech can be distributed along a row of columns or a sequence of rooms. Then he can mentally scan the facade or walk through the building and find what he has stored. The order and regularity of this house makes a helpful contrast with Augustine's account of remembering the past. Here there are tracts of land and vast palaces (*C.* 10.8.12), something like the ground plans of late Roman 'great houses' that archaeologists can reconstruct but find hard to interpret. It is impossible to remember where particular memories are stored, even if one has not forgotten that there was something to look for. Why did Augustine forget about Ambrose's discovery of relics when he was writing book six, then remember it when he was writing about his baptism in book nine (*C.* 9.7.16)? What else has he forgotten (*C.* 4.12.21)? Other memories thrust themselves forward asking, 'Will we do?' A more startling image of memory is the stomach of the mind (*C.* 10.14.21), in which different foods are digested and supply nourishment but do not retain their distinctive taste.

Augustine is not satisfied with the vague terminology of 'memories'. He wants to differentiate memories of events, places, technical terms and emotions, to explain how we can remember what we felt without now feeling the same emotion. In book ten he revives questions he had posed in book one about the use of language. In book one he cannot of course remember learning to talk but he deduces that he did so by interpreting body-language, by trying to use it himself and by linking it with the sounds people made in association with particular objects. Thus he began to take part in human society. Language is stored in his memory, like the objects and concepts associated with language. What he knows and what he says depend on memory. But when he talks of God or of the 'blessed life' (*beata vita*), the happiness that comes from closeness to God, he cannot say that these are 'in' his memory or that he already knows what he is still struggling to understand. 'Memory' comes to include everything a human mind knows or can know, not just the past experience of a human individual. Once again, what interests him in his own experience is not himself remembering – nor what he can retrieve of his past – but the activity of remembering and what it can tell us about human existence in relation to God. 'This is a force of my mind and belongs to my nature, yet I myself do not grasp all that I am' (*C.* 10.8.15). 'All that I am' does not mean subconscious memories that are out of his reach: he means that introspection and reflection on the powers of the human mind is, as the Platonists taught, a way of understanding the true nature of human beings in relation to God.

How do we deal with the jumble of remembered experience? By ordering it into a story, a narrative sequence, which seems to us to make sense and which, in turn, calls up other memories or awareness that something has been forgotten. That is what Augustine has been doing in books one to nine, telling as much as he can of how God brought him back to Christian faith. Readers may like to try the experiment of asking, 'How did I come to be what I am now?' and noticing what they now count as important about themselves, what memories count as explaining it, what might count as a future development of the story. What seems most important – a philosophical position, human relationships, social context, ways of conveying ideas? Is it a Christian, a Marxist, a liberal humanist or a quite other kind of story?

What interests Augustine in books ten to eleven is the content of the question, 'How did I come to be what I am now', the philosophical problems of narrative and time. Narrative is an ordered temporal sequence: this happened, then this, and now ... but what is 'now'? Augustine uses an example, one of Ambrose's hymns, which he quotes several times in *Confessions*. The opening line *Deus creator omnium* ('God creator of all things') appears in an early discussion of transience (*C.* 4.10.15) as an invocation of God's help. The first two verses of the hymn come to Augustine's mind as he wakes from sleep after Monica's death; they help his recovery from grief (*C.* 9.12.32). Now he reflects on the experience of singing, of making successive sounds (*C.* 11.27.35). As he sings *Deus creator omnium*, he moves from one sound to the next, remembering what he has just sung and expecting what he will sing next. The future sound becomes the present and then the past sound. The singer is stretched between what he has done and what he will do; he measures the long and short syllables but cannot measure their duration until they are over. Then they are no longer there to be measured. He cannot explain what he is doing. What is true of singing a hymn is also true, on a larger scale, of human life, so that existence in time disintegrates as he tries to make sense of it. (*C.* 11.28.38-29.39). This is what he has experienced in writing about his life. 'You are my eternal father, but I am dispersed in times whose order I do not know, and my thoughts, the inmost entrails of my soul, are torn apart by the storms of change until I flow together in You, purified and molten by the fire of your love.' The experience of time is *distentio animi*, not just an extension of the spirit over remembered past and expected future but a 'distension', a pulling apart, of the soul.

Telling stories

When we think about it, according to Augustine, existence in time disintegrates, so too does the possibility of narrative, and indeed of any communication. Augustine was acutely aware of the factors that actually convey meaning and cause acceptance, and of the gap between words spoken and their reception: in *The Teacher* he argues that there is no discernible connection between what the teacher says and what the student hears. Nevertheless, like many critics who think communication is strictly impossible, he can order a narrative better than most. He had been trained to select, structure, present, to hold the interest of an audience and to pre-empt, as far as possible, the likely audience reaction. His style proclaims this skill but he also makes it explicit: he will not allow his readers to cast themselves as passive consumers of rhetoric. On the contrary, he first disconcerts them by talking all the time to God (should they be listening?), then reminds them that they are readers of a text and that they are, as human beings, challenged by what is being read. They are not to lapse into the comfortable satisfaction of curiosity. Book ten insists that we think about what it might mean to love God and to try to live as God wants. 'People are curious to know about other people's lives and slack about amending their own. Why do they ask me to tell them who I am, when they do not want You to tell them who they are?' (C. 10.3.3). That is the point of having a human audience for a confession directed to God.

Rhetorical skill, as Augustine also reminds his readers, is suspect. It is a technique bound up with pagan culture and formed on pagan models, as in his own study of Cicero and Virgil: how can anyone use the technique without creating for himself and his readers an intertext of unholy literature and false ideals? Christians in the late fourth century were beginning to convince themselves that they could use the style but transform the content. Yet why should they need the techniques of pagan falsehood to make Christian truth convincing? Readers have been warned to stay alert and not to be taken for a ride. Yet it is very hard not to be caught up in Augustine's own story. It reads like a true and moving account of one man's conversion, but perhaps the story is too good to be true.

Augustine selects, as an archetypal account of human sin, his theft of fruit (C. 2.4.9) from a forbidden tree: not because it was good fruit or because he needed it, but for the satisfaction of breaking the rules. This episode comes in the context of adolescent lust. The critical break with his past life, the moment at which he resolves to live in chastity, comes in a garden under a fig-tree. Augustine hears a voice 'like a child's' (C. 8.12.29) chanting two words of Latin, *tolle lege* ('pick up, collect' in a game, or 'pick up and read'). He takes this as a message from God, opens his book – 'the book of the Apostle', which always means Paul – and finds a verse which summons him to chastity.

So Augustine, who has sinned as Adam did by taking forbidden fruit and has become subject to sexual desire, is rescued under the tree from which Adam and Eve in Genesis took fig leaves to hide their genitals. The words that tell him what he must do are those of Paul, the archetype of the sinner instantly converted: a 'Damascus road experience', such as happened to Paul, is still a familiar phrase. Augustine, whose life had been shaped by the written word, acknowledges that he was looking for a text to change his life. Antony's life had been changed by a text, 'Go, sell all you have and give to the poor, and you shall have treasure in heaven'; and Augustine had just been reminded of Antony by the story Ponticianus told (*C*. 8.6.15) of the civil servants who were converted by reading Antony's life. Is it all too carefully shaped to be true? Augustine dramatised the debate between his old loves and the Lady Continence (*C*. 8.11.26-7): has he done the same to the rest? Has he made a story into a plot?

Fifteen years passed before Augustine wrote *Confessions*. The episode in the Milan garden may have taken on new resonances for him as he thought about it: inevitably he writes in retrospect, looking for the origins of the person he is at the time of writing. A man in his forties, established in a pattern of life, is not likely to see things as he did at thirty-something, when other options were real possibilities. In 386 Augustine responded quite differently to the transformation of his life, living in a peaceful house at Cassiciacum with a group of family and friends, in a modest version of the cultivated leisure (*otium*) enjoyed by Romans who had retired from political activity. In the *Soliloquies* he wrote at the time, talking not to God but to Reason, Augustine considers his own reactions very much in the tradition of moral self-examination. 'So, you have rejected wealth and power but are you quite sure you do not want a charming, cultured wife with just enough money of her own, who would not obstruct your pursuit of philosophy?' The vital text from Paul does not feature in the work of these years; nor, indeed, does Paul feature as the liberated sinner.

This is not to say that nothing happened in a garden at Milan or that nothing happened in the way that Augustine described it in *Confessions*. It is a believable story. Some people do have sudden and dramatic experiences of being freed from compulsion; and the *sortes Biblicae*, the practice of opening the Bible (apparently) at random, usually supplies a verse which can be interpreted to fit the situation. People used to do *sortes Virgilianae* too, with equal success; *sortes Augustinianae* also work. The sample reference in the Preface to this book was provided by *sortes* ('how could she know it was the one she had lost, unless she had remembered it?' *C*. 10.18.27). An even better one was provided for a helpful philosopher, who, like Augustine, finds Aristotle's *Categories* really quite straightforward: 'I was not aware that these arts are extremely difficult even for hard-working and intelligent people to understand, until I tried to explain them' (*C*. 4.16.30).

Augustine describes a mixture of imperceptible process and moment of decision that is also believable. It is like C. S. Lewis' realisation, as he sat on the top deck of a bus in Oxford, that his philosophical position did now imply belief in God – a fact which did not, at the time, encourage him at all. Augustine moves through several stages of conversion, inspired by his reading of *Hortensius* and of the 'Platonic books' and by the example of people he admired (*C*. 8.5.10). Some time elapses between his moment of liberation and his decision to be baptised; further time between his baptism and his decision to lead a monastic life in a community of friends. He was fully capable of seeing or of constructing the narrative patterns that critics have found in his life. But what was theologically vital to him at the time of writing *Confessions* was his liberation from the chains of sin, and specifically from sexual compulsion, by the reading of a biblical text and his God-given response to it. To say 'it could happen' is not to say that it did happen. It may be too good a story to be true but how can we say, against Augustine, that it did not happen? Stories are made by the telling and what needs telling will change over time. 'Time is not empty and does not roll ineffectively through our senses: it does remarkable things to the mind' (*C*. 4.8.13).

Speaking the truth: rhetoric and style

Stories also change over time in the way they are told, in the style and the story-patterns that carry conviction. For those who hold that there is no truth, no final and correct account of anything (is it then true that there is no truth?), what matters is the rhetoric, the persuasive speech that for the moment evokes a response in the audience. For those who hold that there is truth, or at least that some claims can be shown to be false, the techniques of rhetoric may seem unnecessary or even dangerous. Augustine had taught those techniques, but he was committed to believing that uneducated people might understand Christian truth more directly and profoundly than the highly educated. One of the most famous stories of the 'Desert Fathers' contrasts Arsenius, former tutor to the sons of Theodosius I, and a fellow-monk, a (probably illiterate) Egyptian peasant: "'Father Arsenius, how is it that you, with such a good Greek and Latin education, ask this uneducated peasant about your thoughts?". Arsenius replied, "I have a Greek and Latin education but I have not yet learned the alphabet of this uneducated peasant".' (PG 65.89a, Arsenius 6).

The educated speaker loses his authority not because there is no knowledge for him to have but because there is truth and it is only by God's grace, not by his professional skill, that he can help his audience to understand. Christian preachers in late antiquity often advocated simplicity in preference to rhetorical display. Rhetorical skill appealed to the highly educated but their congregations included ordinary working people – and, of course, women – who rarely had more than primary education. Moreover, the study of rhetoric was bound up with the study of pagan authors, whereas the Bible in Greek or in Latin seemed to be written in a quite different style. Classically trained scholars find New Testament Greek on a first encounter disconcertingly naïve, even incorrect; educated men in the fourth century had much the same reaction to the Greek or Latin Scriptures. Augustine takes it for granted that Jesus' disciples were uneducated men, speaking the 'language of fishermen': in *City of God* he uses this as an argument that the spread of Christianity, against all odds, demonstrates its truth. Even the style of Paul, who is by far the most rhetorical of the New Testament writers, could be a problem. Jerome carefully explains that Paul is not really uneducated but is writing in Greek, a language that does not come easily to him, because he thinks in Hebrew. It was only in the twentieth century that the *koine* ('common') Greek of the New Testament was put in the context not of uneducated speech, but of professional non-literary prose.

But the skilled speakers who rejected rhetoric did so with full use of their rhetorical skill. When they preferred *sermo humilis* ('low' style), this was not absence of style but a particular style whose name they had learned from Cicero. *Sermo humilis* is the style of an educated person trying to keep it simple. It is more ordered and coherent than everyday speech, has a carefully chosen vocabulary and carries a risk of condescension. (Ambrose, for example, whose usual preaching style is formal, is an important source of information on ancient wrestling techniques, because he uses wrestling metaphors rather as present-day clergy use football.) Augustine says that his own experience with the Manichaeans taught him that neither fluency nor simplicity is a guarantee of truth: 'I had learned from You that nothing should seem true just because it is eloquently said, or false just because the lips make sounds that are awkward; and again that a thing is not true because it is said without polish, nor false because the style is splendid' (*C.* 5.6.10). He argued in *Christian Teaching* that rhetoric could legitimately be used in the service of Christian truth. It did not require a formal education; for anyone, he said in the maddening way of the very clever, could pick up the rules of grammar and style. The Bible itself uses the major rhetorical techniques, which do not necessarily belong to a corrupt pagan culture. Variation of style is quite proper and does not imply that the speaker thinks some aspects of Christian truth are more important. Sometimes it is necessary to explain, sometimes to convey approval or disapproval, sometimes to 'bend' an audience so that they will behave differently. The 'ordinary' style is better suited to explaining, the exalted style to influencing the audience. The 'moderate' style (*genus temperatum*) is designed to please the audience: this is acceptable provided the speaker's aim is to help his audience to some good, not to show off his own skill. When

Augustine re-read *Confessions*, he noted one passage that seemed to him to fail the test. He had quoted some familiar thoughts on friendship, saying that he and the friend who died at Thagaste were like one soul in two bodies; and he had suggested (*C.* 4.6.11) that he was afraid to die himself because then his friend would have died altogether.

In *Confessions*, Augustine uses all the available 'registers' of style and moves between them with great rapidity, even within a sentence. Some of the most impressive passages depend on very simple vocabulary and syntax arranged with great skill in a setting of much greater elaboration. Here is one famous instance:

> sero te amavi, pulchritudo tam antiqua et tam nova, sero te amavi! et ecce intus eras et ego foris, et ibi te quaerebam, et in ista formosa quae fecisti deformis inruebam. mecum eras et tecum non eram. ea me tenebant longe a te, quae si in te non essent, non essent. vocasti et clamasti et rupisti surditatem meam, coruscasti, splenduisti et fugasti caecitatem meam, fragrasti et duxi spiritum et anhelo tibi, gustavi et esurio et sitio, tetigisti me et exarsi in pacem tuam.

> Too late I loved you, beauty so old and so new, too late I loved you! Look, you were within and I was outside and sought you there, and I rushed, unlovely, upon those lovely things that you made. You were with me and I was not with you. I was kept far from you by things that would not exist if they did not exist in you. You called and cried out and shattered my deafness, you blazed and shone and drove away my blindness, you were fragrant and I drew breath and pant after you, I tasted and am hungry and thirsty, you touched me and I was on fire for your peace.   [*C.* 10.27.38]

Here the rhythm and the vocabulary shift from the deliberately simple ('you were with me and I was not with you') to the consciously grand ('you shattered my deafness, you blazed and shone'). Repetition ('too late I loved you') and word play ('unlovely...lovely', 'would not exist...did not exist') are combined with variation in the responses of the five senses, where both the phrase-length and the tenses change. Such sharp contrasts and changes, coexisting with the inherited classical style, appealed to late antique taste. Visual art shows the same liking for bright and multiple colours, complex and lively patterning and virtuoso display of skill. Augustine has a particular liking for rhyme and assonance, which he uses far more than his classical models would approve. But this is not just an ornament of speech to delight the reader: it is one more device for making the reader take notice. Rhymes, quasi-rhymes and puns came back into literary fashion in the late twentieth century because they raise readers' awareness of how words work (consider 'textual harassment', a useful phrase for the negative presentation of female characters). Augustine is incapable of using a word inattentively. *Confessions* is the book of a man who listens to what he says and tries to understand what it implies both by logic and by association. He will use any available technique to make his readers equally aware of what he is saying and they are reading.

Intertexts: Bible, classical culture and philosophy

All of us bring associations to what we read and respond more willingly to a book, as to a person, if we have associations in common. This often undeclared baggage is the intertext, the reading 'between the lines' which the author cannot control but can try to evoke by quotation or allusion. Classical Greek and Latin literature is quite remarkably intertextual, always in dialogue with earlier texts. The commentary of Servius on the *Aeneid*, written in the late fourth century, shows how students of Augustine's time were trained to be aware of these literary references. In their own speeches they, too, deployed allusion, quoting and evoking the authors of their classical education in order to establish a sense of community with their hearers and to affirm them as educated people. Allusion may enrich one text with resonances and memories of another, as when Virgil used phrases from the earlier Roman epic of Ennius or from his own contemporary Lucretius. It may demonstrate that one author is aware of another, writing in relation to the other text or appropriating it for his own purposes. Late antique Christian poets, such as Prudentius, often appropriated phrases and even whole lines from Virgil, perhaps to show that classical culture and Christianity are compatible, perhaps to demonstrate the triumph of Christianity.

In *Confessions* Augustine takes it for granted that his readers are people like himself. They can hear what he is saying because they are trained to be aware of language and literature, and because the rhythms of Virgil and the Latin Bible are part of their lives, just as Shakespeare and the Book of Common Prayer were for generations of English readers. Even a brief reference ('there is a tide in the affairs of men', 'the husks that the swine did eat') can evoke the unstated context. When Augustine preached, he made constant references to the Bible, starting (usually) from the readings for the day and interpreting them in relation to other parts of Scripture, sometimes in extended quotation, sometimes only by allusion to a familiar phrase or story. Some sections of *Confessions* (e.g. 13.12.13) are almost a *cento* of biblical texts. ('Cento' is Latin for 'patchwork', a fabric made by sewing together pieces of material.) The influence of the Bible extends beyond quotation. The rhythms and idioms of Hebrew prose and poetry, translated into Latin, are essential to Augustine's Latin style in *Confessions*, just as Milton's English style was affected by the Latin constructions he could use so fluently.

As with New Testament Greek, the effect of 'Christian Latin' is disconcerting to the classically trained reader. The most pervasive difference is a preference for linking clauses with 'and', as in Hebrew narrative, rather than subordinating one to another in the manner of classical Latin. This increases the intensity of contrast and movement that is so characteristic of Augustine. 'Too late I loved you', quoted above, is one example. Another brief example comes from Augustine's account of the 'Platonist books':

> et inde admonitus redire ad memet ipsum intravi ad intima mea duce te et potui, quoniam factus es adiutor meus. intravi et vidi ...

> And admonished from there [i.e. the Platonist books] to
> return to myself, I entered my inmost parts led by you,
> and I was able because you had become my helper. I
> entered and saw... [*C*. 7.10.16]

Most of the paragraphs in book seven begin with 'and'. The
subject matter is the impact on Augustine of the Platonic books
and the contrast between Platonist and Christian doctrines. This
sentence begins a chapter that is clearly influenced by Plotinus,
but its style imposes the Bible on Plotinus. Sometimes Plotinus
is brought into line by Bible quotation, a tactic Augustine had
first met in Ambrose's sermons at Milan; sometimes Augustine
transforms what Plotinus says. In the last chapter of book seven
Augustine's impassioned gratitude to God has overwhelmed
his Platonist attempt; and the words of the Bible dominate and
dismiss the books of the Platonists.

> In them no one sings, 'Shall not my soul be subject to
> God? For from him is my salvation; he indeed is my God
> and my saviour, my supporter; I shall not be moved any
> more'. No one there hears him calling, 'Come to me, you
> who labour'. They disdain to learn from him, because
> 'he is meek and lowly of heart'. 'For you have hidden
> these things from the wise and prudent and revealed
> them to the little ones.' And it is one thing to see from a
> wooded summit the homeland of peace, and not to find
> the way to it, and try in vain through pathless places
> while fugitive deserters beset and ambush you with their
> leader 'the lion and the dragon', and another to keep to
> the road which leads there, maintained by the care of
> the heavenly emperor, where those who have deserted
> the army of heaven do not attack like brigands, for they
> avoid it like torture. [*C*. 7.21.27]

A second noticeable effect of Hebrew style is 'parallelism'.
The poetry of the Psalms very often works by making a point,

then restating it in slightly different form. The rhythms are distinctive and preserve some of their effect both in Latin and in English translation. Here is an example, from the psalm Augustine most often cites; the translation is that used in the Book of Common Prayer (1662), because its cadences are both familiar and unfamiliar to (some) present-day English readers, as those of the Latin Bible were to Augustine's audience.

> Like as the hart desireth the waterbrooks: so longeth my
>   soul after thee, O God.
> My soul is athirst for God, yea even for the living God:
>   when shall I come to appear before the presence of
>   God?
> My tears have been my meat day and night; while they
>   daily say unto me, Where is now thy God?
> Now when I think thereupon, I pour out my heart by
>   myself: for I went with the multitude, and brought
>   them forth into the house of God.
> In the voice of praise and thanksgiving among such as
>   keep holy-day.
> Why art thou so full of heaviness, O my soul, and why
>   art thou so disquieted within me?
> Put thy trust in God, and I will yet give him thanks for
>   the help of his countenance.
> [Psalm 42 (41 in Greek and Latin versions) verses 1-7]

It is often illuminating to set out Augustine's text in the same visual form. His Latin prose does not correspond neatly with Hebrew, but there is a structural resemblance. For example, Augustine is baffled by the problem of how we can measure time:

> My soul is on fire to know this thing:
> this most intricate enigma.
> Do not shut them off, O Lord my God, kind father;
> by Christ I implore you, do not shut off from my longing
> these familiar and hidden things;
> so that it might not enter into them
> nor they be illuminated by the light of your mercy, O Lord.

Whom shall I question about these things?
And to whom shall I more profitably confess my ignorance?
My zeal is no annoyance to you
as it blazes in the study of your scriptures. [*C.* 11.22.28]

Hebrew idiom also nurtures Augustine's liking for strongly physical imagery, which may well have been dead metaphor in Hebrew and even in Greek translation but is alive to the point of aggressiveness in Latin. 'Mind' and 'heart' are especially likely to be affected, because they are the homes of thought and emotion. Thus, finding importunate memories thrusting themselves on the attention, 'with the hand of my heart I drive them away from the face of my memory' (*C.* 10.8.12); and earlier Augustine tries (*C.* 4.5.10) to 'move the ear of my heart close to your mouth'. 'Memory is the stomach of the mind' (*C.* 10.14.21), which seems to be Augustine's own invention, almost draws an apology from him. It is, he says, laughable, but not entirely irrelevant, to compare memories of happy or sad things to sweet or bitter food which remains in the stomach but is no longer tasted.

The Bible is the dominant but not the only intertext of *Confessions*. Virgil and the classical cultural tradition also evoke the shared memories of Augustine and his educated readers. Virgil's hexameters cannot successfully form part of a prose text, except in direct quotation. When Augustine relates the conversion of Marius Victorinus, he constructs an immense Ciceronian sentence, heavy with superlatives and subordinate clauses and adorned with a classical tag, to express the status of Victorinus at Rome:

> habet enim magnam laudem gratiae tuae confitendam tibi, quemadmodum ille doctissimus senex et omnium liberalium doctrinarum peritissimus quique philoso-phorum tam multa legerat et diiudicaverat, doctor tot nobilium senatorum, qui etiam ob insigne praeclari magisterii, quod cives huius mundi eximium putant, statuam Romano foro meruerat et acceperat, usque ad illam aetatem venerator idolorum sacrorumque sacrile-gorum particeps, quibus tunc tota fere Romana nobilitas inflata spirabat, [†] popiliosiam [†] et omnigenum

deum monstra et Anubem latratorem, quae aliquando
contra Neptunum et Venerem contraque Minervam tela
tenuerant et a se victis iam Roma supplicabat, quae iste
senex Victorinus tot annos ore terricrepo defensitaverat,
non erubuerit esse puer Christi tui et infans fontis tui,
subiecto collo ad humilitatis iugum et edomita fronte ad
crucis opprobrium.

There is great praise for your grace in confessing to you
how that most learned old man, most expert in all the
liberal arts, who had read and assessed so many writings
of philosophers, teacher of so many noble senators, who
had even earned and been awarded a statue in the Roman
forum, the highest honour in the judgement of the citizens
of this world, because of his exceptional teaching, who
even up to that time of life was a worshipper of idols
and a participant in sacrilegious rites, those that almost
all the Roman nobility sighed after at that time, 'the
many monstrous gods, barking Anubis; against them
Neptune, Venus and Minerva hold spears', the gods that
Rome had defeated and now supplicated, that the old
man Victorinus had for so many years defended with
his awe-inspiring voice; how he did not blush to be the
child of your Christ and an infant from your font, his
head bowing to the yoke of humility and his proud head
submitting to the disgrace of the cross.   [C. 8.2.3]

Latin is an inflected language: word-endings rather than word-
order show the role of a word within a sentence. So Augustine
(unlike this translation) did not find it necessary to resume his
sentence with 'how he did not blush' before the transformation of
Victorinus: he builds it to a triumphant conclusion 'to be the child
of your Christ...he did not blush'. Where the rhythm changes
in English, 'the many monstrous gods', he is quoting Virgil
(*Aeneid* 8.698-700), lightly adapted to fit his sentence but still
recognisably hexameters in Latin. The final phrase on the baptism
of Victorinus includes two brief quotations from the Bible: 'the
yoke of humility' and 'the disgrace of the cross'.

Classical prose is easier to accommodate than verse. When Augustine wrote *Confessions*, the prose rhythms of the classical tradition could not be taken for granted: some literary works were already using the new rhythms called the *cursus*, more suited to Latin as it was then spoken. Augustine remarks in *Christian Teaching* that African speech did not distinguish the long and short vowels that were the basis of classical metre. But the *cursus* does not appear in *Confessions*. As Augustine describes his study of the 'liberal arts', his style becomes smoothly Ciceronian (*C*. 4.16.30); when he tells us how he won a school prize for rhetoric, he moves between the style in which he excelled and a cry of protest against it. The set topic is reported as a hexameter, minimally adapted from Virgil. The requirements are heavily Ciceronian:

> ille dicebat laudabilius, in quo pro dignitate adumbratae
> personae irae ac doloris similior affectus eminebat,
> verbis sententias congruenter vestientibus. ut quid
> mihi illud, o vera vita, deus meus? quid mihi recitanti
> adclamabatur prae multis coaetaneis et conlectoribus
> meis?

> That one spoke most admirably, in whom, according to the status of the character represented, there stood out the most convincing expression of anger and resentment, the words suitably clothing the sentiments. What was this to me, O my true life, my God? Why did my recitation win applause in preference to my many fellow-students and fellow-declaimers?   [*C*. 1.17.27]

This translation aims to bring out Augustine's shift of register. Two Ciceronian sentences, complex in structure and polysyllabic in vocabulary, describe the contest he won by excelling in Virgilian emotion and Ciceronian dignity. They surround a brief, simple, near-colloquial cry to God. Its opening, *ut quid*, is a piece of distinctively Christian Latin, a direct translation from Hebrew idiom. It evokes the Bible and its emotional intensity contrasts with the kind Augustine had so successfully represented. The contestants were to express in prose the feelings of Virgil's

Juno, who attempts to thwart what she knows to be the divine purpose for Aeneas because it threatens her own commitments and disregards her claims for respect as the consort of Jupiter. In the *Aeneid* Juno (like most of the other female characters) is the voice of desire thrust aside: Virgil gives great eloquence to those whose claims he denies, just as Augustine speaks in the voice of the culture he rejects to others who will respond to it.

One other voice is often heard: that of Platonist philosophy, from the books which Augustine was given at Milan or read later. Augustine does not say what exactly the books were and they cannot be certainly identified from his references to their doctrine. Platonist authors commented on one another and many late antique Platonist texts are now known only by name or from a few quotations. It is very likely that the 'Platonist books' included some translations of Plotinus, who taught at Rome in the mid-third century and whose student Porphyry probably continued the tradition into the early fourth century. This conjecture is strengthened by Augustine's style when he is engaged in philosophical speculation rather than exposition. He had read extensively in Cicero's philosophical dialogues and that is the style he uses in *Confessions* for expounding a problem in ethics: does anyone love the crime he commits (*C*. 2.5.11)? What exactly is happening when it seems that two wills are in conflict in one person (*C*. 8.10.24)? But when he is exploring and speculating, he sounds much more like Plotinus.

Plotinus, according to Porphyry, did not give set lectures to expound his philosophical system but preferred discussion with his students. He sometimes circulated the results in the form of short treatises, which Porphyry collected and organised in the *Enneads*. Plotinus offers questions, provisional solutions, objections, revised solutions that raise still further questions; he could also write brilliant inspirational passages. Augustine would have been very happy in Plotinus' seminar, over a century earlier, raising questions which were given all the time they needed. The difference between them is that Augustine constantly appeals for God's help in dealing with questions that may be beyond human understanding or may be obscured by his sin. He lacks the confidence of Plotinus and Porphyry in the attainments of

God-given reason but he tackles philosophical questions in the
same style. Here is Plotinus reflecting on the theory that the soul
may retain memories of previous existence:

> We had better ask first which power of the soul it is
> that remembering accompanies. Is it that by which we
> perceive and by which we learn? Or does remembering
> desirable things also accompany the power by which we
> desire, and remembering things which make us angry
> accompany the assertive power? Yes, someone will say:
> there will not be one thing that enjoys, and another thing
> that remembers what the first thing enjoys. If that is so,
> the desiring power is moved by what it has enjoyed when
> it sees the desired object again – obviously by memory,
> because, if not, why should it not be moved when it sees
> something else, or sees it differently?   [*Ennead* 4.3.28]

And here is Augustine, also reflecting on memory, asking how it
is that he can seek for the happy life, the *beata vita*:

> I do not have it until I say, 'Enough: that's it'. So I ought to
> say how I seek it: by remembering, as if I had forgotten it
> but still recall that I have forgotten, or by an urge to learn
> the unknown, whether that is something I have never
> known or something I have forgotten so completely that I
> do not even remember I have forgotten. Surely the happy
> life is that which everyone wants and there is no one who
> really does not want it? How did they know it to want it
> like that? Where did they see it to love it? We do have it,
> I do not know how. There is another sense in which a man
> is happy at the time when he has it, and there are people
> who are happy in hope. These people have it in a lesser
> form than those who already are happy in the thing itself,
> but they are nevertheless better than those who are happy
> neither in the thing nor in hope. But even they, unless
> they had it in some way, would not want so much to be
> happy: and it is most certain that they do want that.
> [*C.* 10.20.29]

Hearing *Confessions*: translation and reception

Most present-day readers do not bring Cicero and Virgil, Plotinus and the Bible, or the techniques of late antique rhetoric, to their reading of *Confessions*: like Augustine when he embarked on the Bible, they need practice in understanding an unfamiliar style. Their experience of reading also differs from that of Augustine's contemporaries. The modern reader faces a clearly printed page. A Latin text will probably note at the foot of the page any 'variant readings', different words offered in different manuscript copies of the text. The editor chooses from these in accordance with his or her opinion about the reliability of a copyist, about the way errors usually arise in manuscript traditions or about Augustine's style; this is what classicists mean by textual criticism. Sometimes there is no solution and the problematic word or phrase is marked with daggers; there is an example in the account of Victorinus' conversion, quoted above, where a word in the Latin cannot be right. So the modern reader, working through the account of Augustine's conversion (*C.* 8.12.29), knows that there is a choice to be made. A voice 'like that of a boy or girl' called 'take and read, take and read'. Was it in the neighbouring house (*in vicina domo*) or in the divine house (*in divina domo*)? If it was the neighbouring house, this was another instance of an apparently chance happening – a child at play – which Augustine interpreted as fulfilling God's purpose. If it was a voice from heaven, the problem of 'what really happened' becomes more complex.

Fourth-century readers of Augustine could not make this choice, though they knew that manuscript copies were not always reliable. They would have acquired a copy of *Confessions*, probably by asking a friend, as Alypius asked Paulinus for a copy of Eusebius' *Chronicle*. Someone had written it out – probably a trained slave, perhaps a devoted Christian admirer. There were not many copies, so the audience may well not have been readers but listeners to someone reading the text, as in the discussions of Augustine and his friends. The experience of reading and hearing 'in time' and in sequence must have been very vivid for them. Even if they were reading to themselves, they are likely to have 'heard' the written words, just as Augustine did whether he dictated or wrote them. The *Confessions*, he says, are uttered silently to God and aloud to people (*C*. 10.2.2). It is, in fact, very likely that they were spoken aloud, that he dictated them. He was trained to speak fluently, remembering and improvising at need; and dictation helps to explain his amazing output of work and, more important, his extraordinary intensity of style. He could talk to himself, to God and to his imagined audience with a shorthand writer in the corner, instead of drafting and redrafting and checking back; we do not know how much revision he did.

So Augustine – and Augustine's audience – heard the words of *Confessions*. Present-day readers probably hear the words and rhythms when silently reading poetry, but they respond to *Confessions* as prose. In many versions it is quite straightforward prose, because the translator has decided that the most important thing is for the reader to grasp what is being said. So (s)he chooses the 'register' of ordinary professional language, the *sermo humilis*, more often than Augustine does. It is really very difficult nowadays to find a grand style that does not provoke incredulity; life was easier in that respect for the seventeenth century translators who found the rhythms of the King James Bible quite natural. That is not the only difference. Modern texts have word-divisions and punctuation; they are divided into paragraphs and chapters; and when Augustine, without warning, moves from his own words to those of Virgil or the Bible, most modern texts italicise or add quotation marks, even give references. All these visual cues were lacking for readers of the first manuscript copies. (The earliest of these dates from soon after Augustine's death.) The audience Augustine expected had to hear changes in his writing.

Reading aloud was a common practice, especially (then as now) for difficult texts: Ambrose once told Simplicianus that Paul is not really difficult to follow if he is read aloud. Silent reading was also common – or what would life have been like in the great libraries? Augustine's awed description (*C*. 6.3.3) of Ambrose silently reading does not mean that this was a new idea. On the level of ordinary human contact, Augustine and his friends had hoped that Ambrose would draw them into discussion; Ambrose was either unaware of them or was setting an example of concentration, perhaps in the hope that they would go away. On another level of interpretation, it must be important that Ambrose reads but does not speak. Plato said that books are a bad way of doing philosophy, because you cannot argue with a book; Augustine, after long experience of teaching, thought that what one person says has no traceable connection with the flash of understanding in another person. Ambrose, the man who had no time to talk, made it possible by his preaching for the Bible to speak to Augustine; but Augustine himself still had work to do. When he wrote to Ambrose giving in his name for baptism, he asked which books of the Bible – 'which of Your books', he says to God – he should read. Ambrose recommended Isaiah and Augustine tried, then put it aside until he had more practice in understanding the Lord's style (*C.* 9.5.13). The Bible, for Ambrose and Augustine, was for exploration and meditation, not a partner in dialectic. *Confessions* offers images of God's word: the dark forests (*C.* 11.2.3) in which deer move and feed and rest; the dark thicket in which birds find fruit (*C.* 12.28.28); the parchment stretched over us like the firmament of heaven (*C.* 13.15.17).

Augustine wanted to send readers of *Confessions* to the Bible and to reflection on their own lives. He knew that some of them had responded; and over the centuries some have continued to respond. His earliest readers were not all enthusiastic: one recipient wrote a decade later to say the book had stayed in his book-cupboard, because he preferred a more straightforward approach. But in the longer term, *Confessions* is one of the most influential books of western European culture. Until the nineteenth century it was less prominent than *City of God* in the publishing history of Augustine's works but it has never dropped out of sight. It has been endlessly re-used, re-interpreted and simply re-copied. To follow its history would require a large-scale, co-operative research project by people who know about the relevant authors and contexts: all that can be done here is to offer a few indications and examples.

Christian writers have used the *Confessions* for exactly the effect that Augustine noted, to arouse the human mind and emotions towards God. They have found an idiom for prayer, interpreted their own relationship to God in the light of Augustine's and used him to support their theology. People who think partly in fragments of literature find that Augustine offers them the model of a style in which to do it and a sense that there are others like them, whether or not their thought becomes prayer. Classical literature constantly works with quotation, allusion, reminiscence and reworking. Augustine uses these techniques to convey the self and the thought of a person formed by literature. In the history of human self-awareness, *Confessions* stands out for acknowledgement of motivations, both conscious and (at the time) below the conscious level, and of the power of words to determine experience. Augustine did not invent autobiography, or the use of one person's experience to exemplify the human condition, but he transformed the kind of self-description that could be thought or written. Here was a man of high intelligence and good (though not the best) education who, instead of identifying with his reason and belittling lesser concerns, presented himself as full of conflict and uncertainty, convinced of his unworthiness and his dependence on God. The sense of himself is characteristic of late antique ascetic Christians; what is distinctive in *Confessions* is the rhetorical technique that incorporates philosophical theology and the prayer-language of Psalms into brilliantly exciting and varied Latin. There are, on the other hand, hostile responses to *Confessions*. Time changed Augustine from a controversial theologian to an authority and his writings acquired canonical status. Interpretations he had offered were taken out of their context in the world he knew and in his own development, and were made into theological principles that could not safely be challenged. So attacks on 'the church' became attacks on Augustine and *Confessions* can be used to show him up. In the fifth century it was his having a concubine, now it is his sending her away.

Here, then, are some of many strands in the reception of *Confessions*. There are readers who sympathise with Augustine's purpose, who engage with his philosophy and his theology, even when they strongly disagree with some of his judgements. There are those who share his delight in literature and take pleasure in his exploration of its effects. There are also readers for whom Augustine represents not the search for truth and love but repression and denial of truth and love in the name of religion. The latter are often the most curious about Augustine, his experiences and his reactions. It is only fair to say that Augustine stimulated curiosity by his allusions to past and present temptations (for instance *C*. 10.30.41) and that he left curiosity unsatisfied.

The examples that follow do not correspond neatly to these strands. They extend over seven centuries. For Petrarch in the fourteenth century, and for Teresa of Avila in the sixteenth, Augustine interpreted and affirmed their experience as Christians. In the eighteenth century, Jean-Jacques Rousseau used his interpretation of his own life as a conscious challenge to Augustine's account of human nature. In the late nineteenth century Marcel Proust was as fascinated by memory and time as Augustine was, but for quite different purposes and without reference to Augustine. This looks like a trajectory, of gradual disengagement from Augustine; but some brief concluding comments may show how variously *Confessions* continues to be read.

Augustine read classical texts in the normal course of fourth-century education; Petrarch read them in the fourteenth-century rediscovery of the classical world and, for him, Augustine was a source of classical learning, a route especially to Cicero. Like Augustine, he saw a conflict between the culture that appeared as the triumph of human reason and the rival claims of Christian tradition. *Confessions* helped him to see how they could be reconciled. Petrarch had many friends in the (still flourishing) Order of Saint Augustine and it was Denis of Bourg St Sepulcre, who was both an Augustinian religious solitary and a Doctor of the University of Paris, who gave him (around 1333) a pocket copy of *Confessions*. Petrarch carried it with him and his works, especially his letters, are full of allusions and quotations. He saw that Plato and Cicero had helped Augustine to Christ and that some of what they said about God and the soul, contempt for this world and longing for another, could just as well have been written by Ambrose or Augustine. *Confessions* also persuaded Petrarch to modify his opinion of the Bible, as Augustine had done:

> There is another work of Augustine, called *Confessions*,
> divided into thirteen books. In the first nine of these he
> confesses all the errors and faults of his whole life, from
> earliest infancy and his mother's milk; in the tenth, the

surviving remnants of sin and his present state of life; in the last three his uncertainties about Scripture and often his ignorance. By this Confession, if I am any judge, he shows himself to be almost the most learned man ever. If you form the habit of reading this book with concentration and devotion, I hope you will never lack pious and salutary tears, tears of shame. I speak from experience. To encourage you to this reading by the influence of him you love, let me tell you that this book was my way into all the holy scriptures. As a conceited youth I fled them for too long. I thought them lowly and unkempt and unequal to secular literature; I loved the latter too much and despised the former. I had a false opinion of myself; to make a brief confession on my own account, I was inspired by youthful arrogance and, as I now understand, by the prompting of the devil. 'This book changed me' (C. 3.4.7) so much that – I do not say I abandoned my early sins; if only I had abandoned them at my present age! – I learned from it not to despise or detest holy scripture. On the contrary, little by little scripture calmed that revulsion and drew to itself my unwilling ears and reluctant eyes. Finally I began to love those scriptures, to admire and investigate them and to pluck from them perhaps fewer flowers – but certainly more fruit than I did from those writings once so beloved. It would have been disgraceful for a Christian to be wholly unchanged by the eloquence of Augustine, when, as he says in book three, Cicero's *Hortensius* had changed him so much. If you cannot find these *Confessions* elsewhere, I will send you a copy.   [*Letters in Old Age* 8.6]

In this letter Petrarch comes close to identifying himself with Augustine; in his dialogue *Secretum* Augustine is his interlocutor in a conversation witnessed by Truth, challenging him to abandon the ties of earthly love and worldly fame. His conflicts are expressed in a very Augustinian letter to his friend Denis (*Letters to Friends* 4.1) – so Augustinian, in fact, that many people have doubted whether the episode he described can really have taken place. Like Augustine's account of his conversion, it was written – or edited – many years after the event and it is almost too good a story to be true. In 1336 Petrarch and his brother climbed with great difficulty to the summit of Mont Ventoux near Valchiusa. He began to reflect, in Augustinian style, on the ten years since he had left university at Bologna, on his own conflicts and frustrations: 'What I used to love, I do not now love; I lie – I do love – but too little. No, I have lied again: I love, but with too much shame and sadness; at last I have told the truth. That is how it is: I love – but something that I would love not to love, that I would want to hate; I love, but unwilling, forced, sad, grieving'. His attention moved between the earthly beauty all around him and thoughts of higher things. Then he opened his copy of *Confessions*, intending to read whatever he found and, like Augustine in the garden at Milan, he found a text: 'People go and admire the heights of mountains and the vast waves of the sea and great waterfalls and the circuit of Ocean and the orbits of the stars, but they leave out themselves' (*C.* 10.8.15).

Two centuries on, another committed Christian found that *Confessions* offered an interpretation of her life. Teresa of Avila did not experience the conflict between classics and Christianity, because, like most women of her time, she had no formal education. She, like Augustine, is a Doctor of the Church but she was recognised as such only in 1970. She began her autobiography in 1562 at the request of her confessor, who thought it would be helpful to him and to her fellow-nuns to hear about the special favours God had given her in response to prayer. She said that she could not write a proper literary style – and this is not false modesty: what she writes is not an elegantly simple *sermo humilis* but loosely constructed, colloquial and sometimes quite difficult to interpret. Only her frequent exclamations in praise of God resemble the style of *Confessions*. She had no training in theology or philosophy and she does not reflect, as Augustine does, on the implications of what she says. Yet her *Life* is in many ways very close to *Confessions* and she acknowledges that *Confessions* changed her life.

Teresa's *Life* was intended for private and very limited circulation to those who might benefit from it. Inevitably other people read it, and it was caught up in controversies about the reform of religious orders and the dangers of interior prayer. She modified and added to the Life in response to comments from other members of religious orders. In its present form it has nine chapters of autobiography, in which she narrates her life with more detail than Augustine but in a very similar tone. She praises her parents but comments on the defects of her upbringing (it must be very difficult to bring up a saint); she grieves over wickedness that the less saintly reader – like her own confessor – finds hard to detect. She and her favourite brother used, as children, to read the lives of the saints and decided to win martyrdom by going to convert the Moors; frustrated in this, they took to playing hermits in the orchard, except that the hermitages would keep falling down. She suggests – but so cryptically that it is difficult to be sure – that she experienced strong sexual desires, and she reports the devastating illness from which she suffered in her early years as a nun. Her nausea and paralysis must have been partly psychosomatic; for in later life, when she had to travel and negotiate to set up a reformed Carmelite order, her health was much better.

The tenth chapter of Teresa's *Life*, like book ten of *Confessions*, is transitional: it introduces thirty chapters that deal with her experience of mental prayer. Chapter nine, like Augustine's book nine on his baptism, deals with the turning point in her life, sometimes called her second conversion. It came when she was given a copy of *Confessions*. If this was the Spanish translation dedicated to a friend of hers in 1554, she was perhaps in her early forties at the time of this episode and had been a nun for twenty years. 'So my soul went on weary and, although it wanted to rest, the wretched habits that it had would not allow it to.' Her way of prayer was changed by an image of Christ wounded; like Augustine, she was given at this critical time the book that she needed.

> Then in that time I was given the *Confessions* of St Augustine, which it seems the Lord ordained, because I did not ask for them and had never seen them. I am very devoted to St Augustine, because the convent where I lived as a secular (i.e. before she became a nun) was of his Order. and also for having been a sinner, because I

found great comfort in the saints whom the Lord had turned to Himself after they had been so. I thought there was help to be had from them and, because the Lord had pardoned them, He might do it for me; except that one thing discouraged me, as I have said: that the Lord had called to them only once and they had not gone back to falling, while I had done it so often that it distressed me. Yet thinking of the love that held me, I would return to confidence, because I never lost faith in His mercy; I often did in myself.

Oh, God help me, how the hardness of my soul amazes me after so much help from God! It frightens me to think how little I could do for myself and how tied down I was so as not to resolve to give myself wholly to God. When I began to read the *Confessions*, I seemed to see myself there and I began to commend myself often to that glorious saint. When I reached his conversion and read how he heard a voice in the garden, it seemed just as if the Lord said it to me, as my heart felt. I was for a long time all dissolved in tears and was in great affliction and distress. Oh, how a soul suffers, God help me, from losing the freedom it had, to be its own master; what torments it endures! It amazes me now that I could live in such torment; praised be God who gave me life to come out of such fatal death!

In *Confessions* Augustine had refused to present his life as conversion followed by instant sanctity. His acknowledgement of continuing weakness and need for God's help gave hope to Teresa, though other readers have vehemently rejected his account of flawed human nature. Jean-Jacques Rousseau called his own autobiography *Confessions* in deliberate reference to Augustine. Describing himself in a letter to the Archbishop of Paris, who had condemned his book *Emile*, he quoted Augustine on the need to tell the truth. He begins his own *Confessions* not with a meditation on God but with a declaration about himself; he presents himself not as an example of human life in relation to God but as a uniquely interesting human being.

I want to show my fellow men a man in all the truth of his nature; that man will be myself – me alone. I know my heart and I know men. I am not made like any of those I have seen; I venture to believe that I am not made like any of those who exist. If I am not worth more, at least I am other. Whether nature did well or badly to break the mould in which she cast me, no one can judge until after reading me. Let the last trump sound when it will, I shall come with this book in my hand to present myself before the sovereign judge. I shall say distinctly: 'this is what I did, what I thought, what I was'. I have said good and bad with the same frankness. I have kept silent about nothing bad and added nothing good ... I have shown myself as I was, contemptible and vile when I was so; good, noble, sublime when I was so. I have unveiled my inner self as you have seen it yourself. Eternal Being, gather round me the innumerable crowd of my fellow-men: let them hear my *Confessions*; let them groan over my unworthy acts and blush for my sufferings. Let each in his turn reveal his heart before your throne with the same sincerity; and let a single one say, if he dares, 'I was better than that man'.

Augustine would never have declared himself good, noble, sublime. Rousseau has other standards of human conduct. He does not confess to God but to other human beings. He offers several motives for these *Confessions*: to relieve his mind, to give readers some knowledge of a human being other than themselves, to refute accusations, to enjoy his memories of himself. But his purpose is to challenge the way his readers think about human life.

Like Augustine, Rousseau sees childhood as a critical time of life. He rejects Augustine's version of the 'cradle argument', in which babies demonstrate the greed, and the desire to dominate, which since the Fall has been innate in the human race. Rousseau believes in original goodness, not original sin: human beings naturally want to survive and prosper but they have no wish to harm others and do not want to see others suffer. According to Rousseau children go wrong not because of inherited sin but because their innate good feelings are corrupted by social hypocrisy and convention. They could, in theory, be reared without corruption, though Rousseau entirely failed to try that out. He wrote about ideal education but handed over his own children to foundling hospitals.

Augustine stole pears that he neither needed nor wanted, and he uses this episode to show the human tendency to sin for nothing else but the sheer satisfaction of breaking the rules and going with the crowd. Rousseau stole apples because he was hungry and because he had started stealing to oblige a fellow-apprentice.

> That is how I learned to covet in silence, to hide myself, to dissimulate, to lie, finally to steal – an idea which had not come to me until then and from which I have never since been able to cure myself entirely. Desire and powerlessness always lead to that. That is why all lackeys are rogues; and why all apprentices should be. But in tranquil and just conditions, when everything they see is within their reach, most apprentices lose this shameful tendency as they grow up. Not having had the same advantages, I could not derive the same profit from them. It is almost always good feelings badly directed which make children take the first steps towards evil. Despite constant privation and temptation, I had stayed over a year with my master without being able to bring myself to take anything, even things to eat. My first theft was a matter of being obliging but it opened the door to others that had not such a laudable purpose.

Rousseau confronts and rejects Augustine's account of human life; Proust shares Augustine's concerns for literature and time and memory, but with no detectable reference to Augustine. Perhaps he read *Confessions* at the Lycée Condorcet, where he was (like Augustine) educated in literature and philosophy, but he does not mention it. *A la Recherche du Temps Perdu* is concerned with the activity of memory, especially involuntary memory, with changing perceptions over time and with the use of literature to interpret experience, especially the experience of love. (Proust differs from Augustine in acknowledging the influence of music and painting as well as literature: Swann's passion for Odette is strengthened because a pose of her head and neck reminds him of women in the paintings of Botticelli.) Like Augustine, Proust realises in retrospect what the direction of his life has been, and investigates the relationship of life to literature and the contents of his memory:

Then a new light occurred in me, less dazzling, to be sure, than that which had shown me that a work of art was the only way to rediscover lost Time. And I understood that all these materials for a work of literature were my past life; I understood that they had come to me, in frivolous pleasures, in laziness, in affection, in suffering, stored up by me without my guessing at their destination, their very survival, any more than the seed putting in reserve all the foodstuffs which will nourish the plant. Like the seed, I could die when the plant had developed, and I found that I had lived for it without knowing, without its seeming to me that my life ought ever to come in contact with those books I should have liked to write, for which, when I used to sit down at my table, I could find no subject. So all my life up to this day could, and could not, have been summed up under the heading: a Vocation. It could not, in the sense that literature had played no part in my life. It could, in that this life, the memories of its sadnesses and of its joys, formed a reserve like the albumen in the ovule of plants, from which the ovule draws its nourishment to transform itself into a seed, at the time when it is still unknown that the embryo of a plant is developing, though the embryo is nevertheless the site of chemical and respiratory phenomena, secret but very active. Thus my life was in touch with that which would bring about its maturation.

Like Augustine, Proust narrates his life, then halts the narrative while he reflects on its implications for his primary concerns. His narrative presents the detail of social relationships and his primary concerns have the same names as Augustine's, but they are quite different. 'Love' means human love; the 'time' that is lost is past human experience. The human past, including the past self (or selves) of a human being, is destroyed by the passage of time but can be saved by literature, especially by the creation of new metaphors that make a fresh connection between sensation and memory. Memory, for Proust, works quite differently from memory in Augustine. His early work *Jean Santeuil* offers the image of the past as an archive of photographs, which may fall open at some forgotten episode. This comparison was not, of course, open to Augustine but it is odd that Augustine never thinks of painting as a kind of memory. For Augustine memories are jumbled up, half forgotten, nourished by reading and experience which has been digested and has lost its specific flavour. Involuntary memory may come but it is not invoked in its totality by a repeated experience, as in the famous case of Proust eating a 'madeleine' dipped in lime tisane.

Augustine and Proust have fundamentally different purposes. Like Augustine, Proust thinks we must go into ourselves to find the real world. Yet that real world is our memories of time past, not the ascent of reason towards God. Proust's father was a practising Catholic but God is nowhere in Proust's work and, if he quotes the Bible, it is as a literary allusion. In *Le Temps Retrouvé* he moves from the image of the 'seed which dies' to its biblical archetype:

> I said to myself not only 'Is there still time?' but 'Am I in any state to do it?' The illness which had done me a service in making me – like a harsh director of conscience – die to the world ('for if the grain of wheat does not die after it is sown, it will be alone, but if it die, it will bear much fruit'), the illness which, after laziness had protected me from facility, would perhaps guard me from laziness, the illness had used up my strength and, as I had long since noticed, especially at the moment when I stopped

loving Albertine, the strength of my memory. Now the recreation by memory of impressions, which must then be deepened, illuminated, transformed into equivalent understanding, was not that one of the conditions, almost the very essence of the work of art as I had conceived it just now in the library?

Proust does not rely on any strength but his own; immortality, for him and his remembered past, can only come from literature.

This sequence of snapshots is not a trajectory moving away from engagement with Augustine. New translations of *Confessions* continue to appear and new interpretations of Augustine continue to be offered. Born at Thagaste, now Souk Ahras, he has recently been proclaimed as Augustine the Algerian. A best-selling author, Jostein Gaarder, has written a letter to Augustine from his concubine (he calls her Floria Aemilia), reproaching him for turning away from human love and the beauty of the world. Augustine is the subject of a film for which *Confessions* will no doubt supply a story line. Thanks to James O'Donnell, Augustine was the first saint to have a home page on the internet ('on the internet nobody knows you're a saint'). Theologians and philosophers continue to discuss Augustine's theology and his arguments on time, memory and language. Literary critics exploit his awareness of the activities of writing and reading. Historians of culture ask whether it was Augustine who discovered the individual. Debates continue on Augustine's own choices and what they imply about human nature in relation to others and to God.

Augustine recognised the multiplicity and endlessness of human interpretation. He wanted readers to use his book to look at themselves. They have done so, though not always in the sense he meant it. Some have looked at themselves in the sight of God; others have looked at their own image and their own preoccupations, finding and taking what they need. I shall end by taking something for myself and for others who, like Augustine, follow the profession of teaching and try to sort out their priorities:

I shall set my feet on the step where my parents placed me
as a child, until the plain truth is discovered. But where
is it to be found? When is it to be found? Ambrose has
no time; there is no time for reading. Where do I look for
the books? Where or when do I buy them? Who would
lend them? There must be set times and hours assigned
for the health of the soul .... My students occupy the
morning hours: what do I do with the rest? Why not this?
But when do I visit the important people whose support
I need? When do I prepare material for the students to
buy? When do I restore myself by relaxing my mind
from its preoccupations?   [C. 6.11.18]

Guide to Further Reading

The periodical *Revue des Études Augustiniennes* includes an annual up-date of work on Augustine in several languages: this runs to sixty or so pages, several of which are always on *Confessions*. These suggestions for further reading are deliberately brief and, with great regret, restricted to English: Augustinian scholarship is multi-lingual but present-day teachers may not be. All items listed, except the older translations, have extensive bibliographies of their own. James O'Donnell's web page

http://www.ccat.sas.upenn.edu/jod/augustine

has links to many resources for the study of *Confessions*, including an out-of-copyright translation and O'Donnell's own *Augustine: Confessions*, a new critical edition of the Latin text with two volumes of commentary (Oxford 1992). This commentary has transformed study of *Confessions* by making Augustine his own commentator, using his own writings, especially his sermons, to illuminate what he says in *Confessions*. The commentary is invaluable, especially for readers who have Latin. Those who do not can still appreciate the comments on specific passages and the longer discussions of important questions, such as Augustine on memory.

Translations are works of interpretation, and two recent translations of *Confessions* deserve to join Henry Chadwick's outstandingly helpful version (Oxford 1991). Philip Burton (Everyman 2001) is a an expert on the Latin of the Bible that Augustine read; his appendix 'On translating Augustine' is the first stage of a full-length study (in preparation) of Augustine's use of language. Maria Boulding, a Benedictine nun who lives as a hermit, contributed *Confessions* (1997) to the splendid series *Augustine for the Twenty-First Century*, produced by the Order of St Augustine (series ed. John A. Rotelle OSA). A much-loved translation by F.J.Sheed (Sheed and Ward, London and New York 1943) was reissued in 1993 (Hackett, Indianapolis), with an introduction by Peter Brown (who notes [xii] that Sheed dictated his translation in an attempt to retain the oratorical quality of Augustine's Latin).

Earlier translations have an interest and charm of their own, especially those based on the seventeenth-century versions in which the rhythms of the King James Bible are very close to the rhythms of ordinary prose. The pioneering work of Sir Tobie Matthew (1624) was revised by William Watts (1631) and many times since; E.B. Pusey's version (1838), once described as 'incense-wreathed', is in effect a new translation. A further revision of Watts appears in the Loeb Classical Library (London 1912) with a facing Latin text.

Among Augustine's many other works, *Christian Teaching* (*de doctrina Christiana*) is especially important for his ideas about rhetoric and interpretation of texts. A lucid, annotated translation by Roger Green is available in Oxford World's Classics (1997). *City of God* (*de civitate Dei*) is available in two good modern translations: Henry Bettenson (Penguin 1972, reissued 2003) and R.W.Dyson (Cambridge 1999). Gerard O'Daly's *Augustine's City of God: a Reader's Guide* (Oxford 1999) is a brilliant concise introduction. There is a lively translation of Augustine's sermons by Edmund Hill O.P. in the series *Augustine for the Twenty-First Century*.

Social and Intellectual Context

Peter Brown: *Augustine of Hippo: a Biography* (London 1967) transformed awareness of Augustine, who was then studied chiefly as a theologian, by presenting him as a man of the late antique world. The revised edition (2000) has two long additional chapters on new evidence (the letters discovered by J. Divjak and the sermons discovered by F. Dolbeau) and new perspectives that have appeared in the last thirty years. Serge Lancel: *St Augustine* (English tr., London 2002) is another wonderfully vivid and detailed account, different in tone, drawing on long study of Augustine's theology and of North African topography and archaeology.

Two important books on the transformation of culture in late antiquity are Robert Markus: *The End of Ancient Christianity* (Cambridge 1990) and Averil Cameron: *Christianity and the Rhetoric of Empire* (Berkeley, Ca. 1991).

Theology and Philosophy

Carol Harrison: *Augustine: Christian Truth and Fractured Humanity* (Oxford 2000) is an excellent introduction to Augustine's theology in the context of the transition from classical to Christian culture. John Rist: *Augustine: Ancient Thought Baptized* (Cambridge 1994) explains his thought in relation to Graeco-Roman philosophy. Readers who wish to try Plotinus will find the translation by A.H. Armstrong in the Loeb Classical Library (7 vols., London 1966-88*)* more lucid than the triumph of style in Stephen MacKenna's version (London 1917-30; revised ed. 1956*)*. The abridgement of MacKenna by John Dillon in Penguin Classics, *Plotinus: the Enneads* (Harmondsworth 1991*)* has very useful editorial material.

John Burnaby: *Amor Dei* (London 1938, reissued 1991) and Gerald Bonner: *St Augustine of Hippo: Life and Controversies* (London 1963, new ed. 1986) both give detailed attention to theology. F. van der Meer: *Augustine the Bishop* (English tr., London and New York 1961, reprinted 1983) affectionately and vividly presents Augustine's pastoral work as priest and bishop of Hippo.

Three deliberately concise studies of a very big subject are Henry Chadwick: *Augustine* (Oxford 1986, reissued as *Augustine: A Very Short Introduction*); James O'Donnell: *Augustine* (Boston 1984); and Richard Price: *Augustine* (London 1996). *Augustine through the Ages: An Encyclopedia*, ed. Allan Fitzgerald OSA (Grand Rapids, Michigan 1999) and the *Cambridge Companion to Augustine*, ed. Eleonore Stump and Norman Kretzmann (Cambridge 2001) will provide further guidance.

Language and Style

Robert Kaster: *Guardians of Language: the Grammarian and Society in Late Antiquity* (Berkeley, Ca. 1988).

Sabine MacCormack: *The Shadows of Poetry: Vergil in the Mind of Augustine* (Berkeley, Ca. 1998).

Michael Roberts: *The Jeweled Style: Poetry and Poetics in Late Antiquity* (Ithaca and London 1990).

Brian Stock: *Augustine the Reader* (Belknap, Harvard 1996) devotes four chapters to Augustine's progress as a reader in *Confessions* 1-9.

Lives and saints' lives

M. Edwards and S. Swain (eds): *Portraits* (Oxford 1997) – a collection of papers on classical and late-antique biography. Swain's wide-ranging introduction includes claims about the discovery of the individual.

T. Hägg and P. Rousseau (eds): *Greek Biography and Panegyric in Late Antiquity* (Berkeley, Ca. 2001) – papers on lives of philosophers, saints and the imperial family.

T. Heffernan: *Sacred Biography: Saints and their Biographers in the Middle Ages* (Oxford 1988), including discussion of late antiquity.

John Sturrock: *The Language of Autobiography: Studies in the First Person Singular* (Cambridge 1993) ranging from Augustine to the twentieth century.

Carolinne White: *Early Christian Lives* (Penguin 1998) translates the lives of Antony and others with helpful introduction and annotation.

Other Members of the Great Fourth-century Generation:

Ambrose: Neil McLynn: *Ambrose of Milan* (Berkeley, Ca. 1994) for political and social setting; Boniface Ramsey OP: *Ambrose* (London 1997) for translations of selected texts.

Basil: Philip Rousseau: *Basil of Caesarea* (Berkeley, Ca. 1994) and Raymond Van Dam: *Kingdom of Snow: Roman Rule and Greek Culture in Cappadocia* (Philadelphia, Pa. 2002) for different perspectives.

Jerome: J.N.D. Kelly: *Jerome: his Life, Writings and Controversies* (London 1975); Stefan Rebenich: *Jerome* (London 2002) for translations of selected texts.

John Chrysostom: J.N.D. Kelly: *Golden Mouth: the Story of John Chrysostom, Ascetic, Preacher, Bishop* (London 1995); Wendy Mayer and Pauline Allen: *John Chrysostom* (London 2000) for translations of selected texts.

Julian: Polymnia Athanassiadi: *Julian and Hellenism* (London 1992); Rowland Smith: *Julian's Gods* (London 1995).

Paulinus of Nola: Dennis Trout: *Paulinus of Nola* (Berkeley, Ca. 1999); Catherine Conybeare: *Paulinus Noster* (Oxford 2000).

Index